Leica Q3 Instructional Handbook

A User-friendly Guidebook Tailored to Assist Q3 Owners in Mastering their Camera's Features

By

Harry Bass

Table of Content

INTRODUCTION

Leica Camera AG proudly presents the third generation of the highly successful Leica Q series, the Leica Q3. This new addition to the family of fixed focal length full-frame cameras continues the legacy of high-quality craftsmanship, timeless design, and user-friendly operation that sets it apart in the world of premium photography. The Leica Q3 redefines excellence in both photography and videography, equipped with cutting-edge features and one of the fastest lenses on the market, complete with an integrated macro mode.

At the core of the Leica Q3 is the revolutionary BSI-CMOS sensor featuring Triple-Resolution-Technology. This groundbreaking technology allows users to choose resolutions of 60, 36, or 18 MP, capturing raw images in the DNG format and pristine JPEG files straight out of the camera. The sensor's sensitivity range spans from ISO 50 to 100,000, utilizing the latest Maestro Series processor with L2 Technology to ensure seamless operation and exceptional processing speeds.

The Leica Summilux 28 mm f/1.7 ASPH. lens, a true optical masterpiece, takes center stage. With an integrated macro mode, it enables close-up shots from a remarkable minimum focusing distance of 6.69 inches. The lens, combined with the high-resolution sensor, introduces an extended digital zoom, allowing creatives to explore focal lengths of 28, 35, 50, 75 mm, and now even 90 mm. Leica Perspective Control (LPC) and Leica Dynamic Range (LDR) assist in delivering perfect JPEG images without the need for post-processing.

The Leica Q3 excels in video recording, boasting 8K resolution and efficient codecs like H.265 and Apple's ProRes. USB-C and HDMI ports facilitate direct connection of external devices, expanding the camera's versatility. Tethered shooting with Capture One or Adobe Lightroom plug-ins is supported via USB-C, further enriching the camera's capabilities.

Wireless charging becomes a reality with the introduction of the new Leica Charging Pad and a separate camera handgrip, providing convenient recharging for the powerful BC-SCL6 battery.

Photographers and videographers can personalize their experience with four function buttons on the Leica Q3, while a range of accessories, including leather protectors, lens caps, retro-look lens hoods, thumb rests, soft release buttons, and flash shoe covers, offer versatility in both appearance and functionality. The accessories are available in three different color variations, allowing users to express their creative vision with style.

CHAPTER 1: GETTING THE CAMERA UP AND RUNNING

Preparing the Camera for Initial Use

How To Set Up The Leica Q3 Camera

Here's how to set up your new Leica Q3 camera when you're feeling stressed:

1. Charge your Leica Q3 camera's battery with the provided charger.

2. Insert a memory card into the camera's SD card slot.

3. Turn on your camera by pressing the power button on the top.

4. Set the time, date, and language in the camera's menu.

5. Adjust focus using the focus ring on the camera lens for photos or movies.

6. Choose shooting settings like scene mode, manual, or auto.

7. Use the touchscreen or buttons to adjust settings like ISO, shutter speed, and aperture.

8. Press the shutter button to frame your shot using the LCD or electronic viewfinder.

9. View your photos by clicking the play button on the camera.

10. Connect your Leica Q3 to your computer or mobile device to transfer and edit photos.

Attaching a Carrying Strap

1. Find the small metal loops on both camera sides near the bottom.

2. Put one strap end through a loop, ensuring it's securely closed. Do the same for the other loop.

3. Adjust the strap to the length you want.

Ensure the camera strap is tightly attached and the clips are secure to prevent the camera from falling.

Charging the Camera

Set Up The Leica Q3 Camera Charger

Plug the charger into the wall using the cord and the correct plug for your area. The charger will adjust to the local power automatically.

How To Charge The Battery For A Leica Q3 Camera

After you follow the steps to charge, use the uncharged lithium-ion battery to power up your Leica Q3 camera.

Make sure the groove faces up when you put the battery in the charger, and press the contacts together.

Press down on the battery until you hear and feel it snap into place. Check the charger to confirm that the battery is charging.

Charging Your Leica Q3 Camera Via USB

The camera's battery charges automatically when connected to a computer or power source using a USB cable. Make sure the factory setting is set to "ON." To adjust USB charging, go to the main menu, find Camera setups, and choose "ON" or "OFF" under USB Charging.

Make sure to charge the camera's battery with a 9.0V/3.0A converter while the camera is on. You can use a lower-rated adaptor, but the battery will slowly lose power. The camera will automatically start recharging.

How To Install Or Remove the Battery In Your Leica Q3

Make sure to switch off the camera. For more details, check out how to turn off your Q3 camera.

Install the Battery

Place the battery in the slot with the groove facing the LCD panel and wait for it to snap into place.

Remove the Battery

1. Flip the switch to let the battery come out a bit.

2. Push the battery down a little, and it will fully open up.

3. Remove the battery.

If you remove the battery while the camera is on, you might lose your settings or harm the memory card.

Inserting/Removing the Memory Card

The camera will store pictures on an SD (Secure Digital), SDHC (High Capacity), or SDXC (eXtended Capacity) memory card.

Inserting the memory card

1. Move the cover like the picture until it clicks. The cover will go up by itself.

2. Insert the memory card with the contacts facing the screen until it clicks.

3. Close and press the cover down.

4. Slide the cover like in the picture until you hear a click.

Removing the memory card

1. Slide the cover like the picture until it clicks. The cover will lift on its own.

2. Press the card until it clicks. The card will come out a bit.

3. Take out the memory card.

4. Shut up and keep the cover down. Slide it as in the picture until it clicks firmly into position.

Note: Different companies sell SD/SDHC/SDXC memory cards in various sizes and speeds for storing data. Cards with more storage and faster speeds store and process data quickly. The camera will show a message if a memory card isn't supported or needs formatting. Ensure the card is aligned correctly if you're having trouble putting it into the camera.

Attaching/Detaching The Lens Hood

This camera comes with a lens hood that's already attached. Using the lens hood is suggested to lessen vignetting.

Detaching

Turn the lens hood to the left to unscrew it, then attach the thread protection ring by screwing it on.

Attaching

- Turn the thread protection ring to the left to unscrew it.

- Twist the lens hood to the right until it stops to attach it.

Note: The lens hood cover can only be used with the hood and not alone. If you want a lens cover without the hood, you can get the optional lens front cap E49 (Order No. 14001) here: https://store.leica-camera.com.

Diopter Settings

Adjust the viewfinder for glasses:

1. Push the diopter wheel until it clicks to unlock it.

2. Look through the viewfinder and focus on an object.

3. Push the diopter wheel back until it clicks to set it in place.

Shutter Button

The shutter button has two steps:

1. Lightly tapping activates the camera electronics, displays, and handles exposure lock.

2. Pressing it fully releases the shutter, saves data to the memory card, and starts video recording, self-timer, or continuous shooting.

Press the shutter button smoothly until you hear a click to avoid shaky photos. The button stays locked if the memory card is full, the battery is not performing well, the card is protected or damaged, or the sensor is too hot.

Date/Time

Date

Pick how you want the date to show up by following these steps:

1. Go to Camera Settings in the main menu.

2. Choose Date & Time.

3. Pick Date Setting.

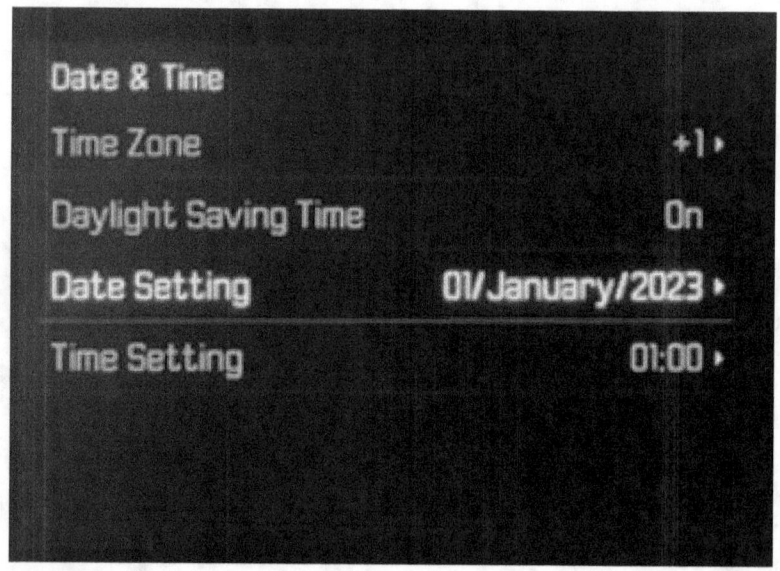

4. Select the date format you prefer (Day/Month/Year, Month/Day/Year, Year/Month/Day).

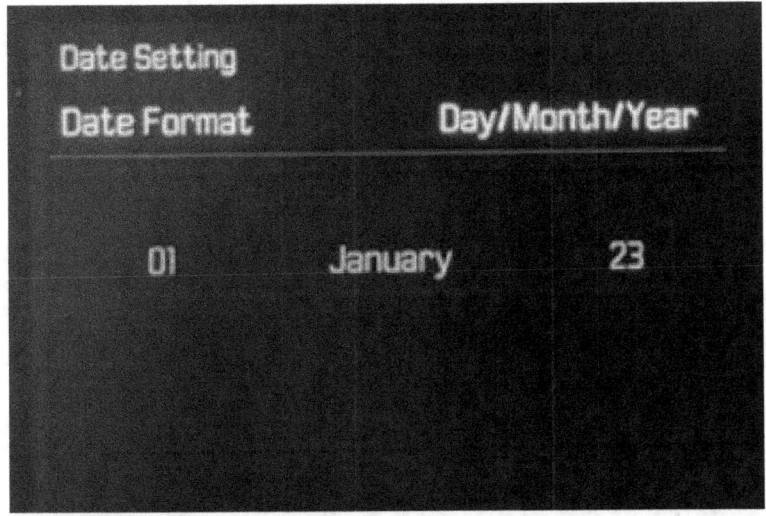

5. Set the date.

Time

1. Go to the main menu and choose "Camera Settings."

2. Pick "Date & Time" from the options.

3. Select "Time Setting."

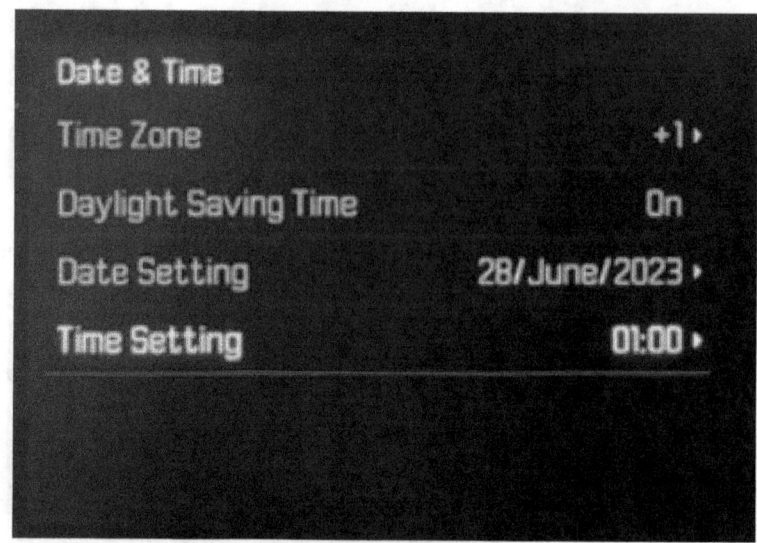

Date & Time
Time Zone   +1 ›
Daylight Saving Time   On
Date Setting   28/June/2023 ›
Time Setting   01:00 ›

4. Choose your preferred brightness format (either 12 Hours or 24 Hours).

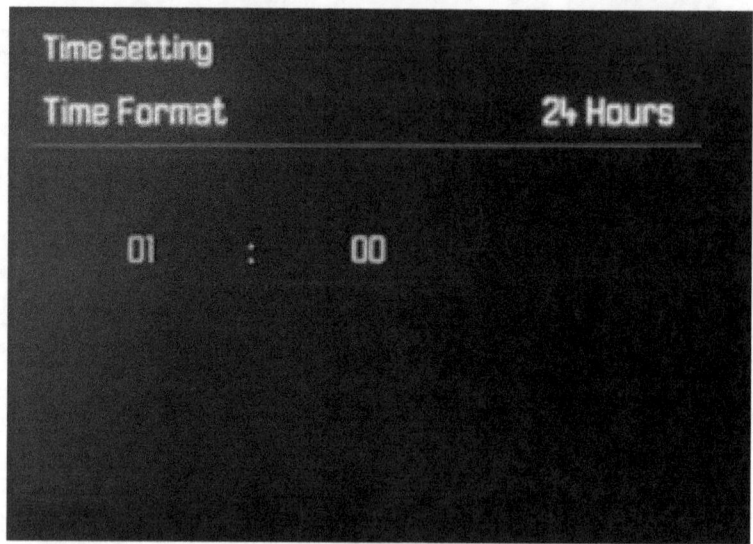

Time Setting
Time Format   24 Hours

      01   :   00

5. Set the time by selecting "am" or "pm" using the 12-hour format.

Time Zone

1. Go to the main menu and choose "Camera Settings."

2. Pick "Date & Time" from the options.

3. Select "Time Zone" and choose your current location.

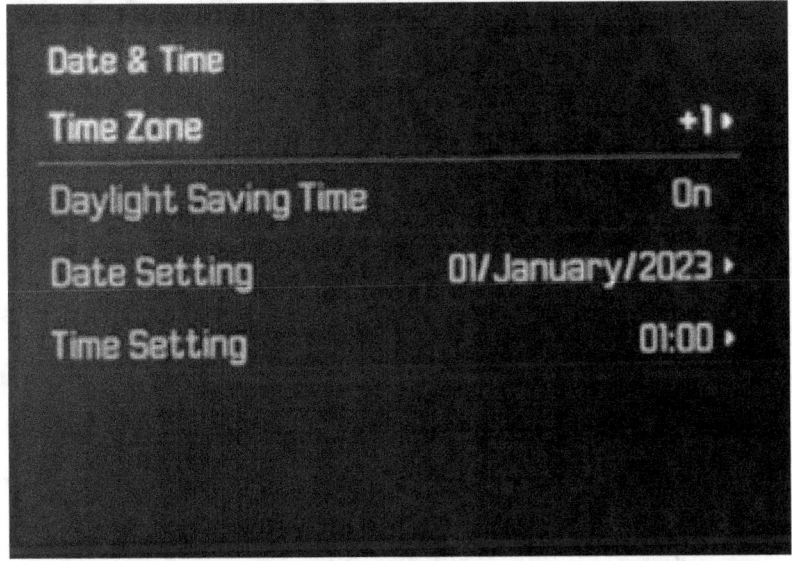

4. The Greenwich Mean Time offset is on the left side, and major cities in that time zone are on the right.

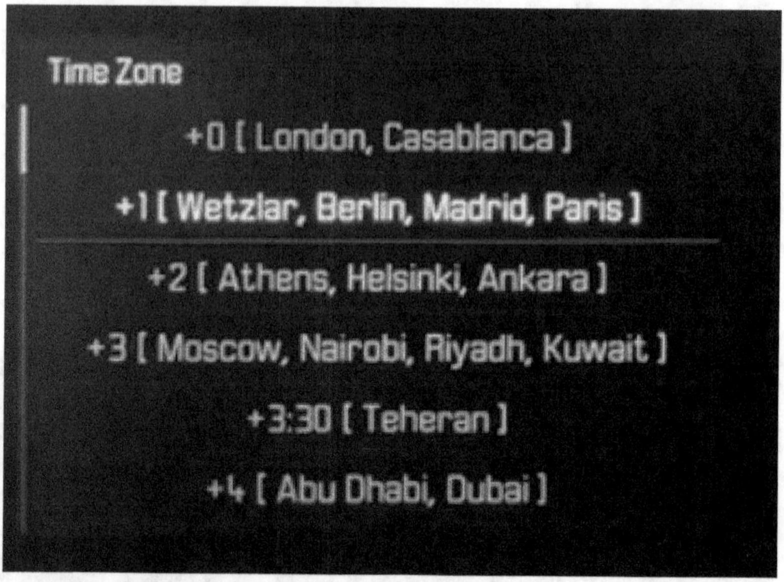

Time Zone

+0 [London, Casablanca]

+1 [Wetzlar, Berlin, Madrid, Paris]

+2 [Athens, Helsinki, Ankara]

+3 [Moscow, Nairobi, Riyadh, Kuwait]

+3:30 [Teheran]

+4 [Abu Dhabi, Dubai]

Daylight Saving Time

1. Go to the main menu and choose "Camera Settings."

2. Select "Date & Time."

3. Choose "Daylight Saving Time."

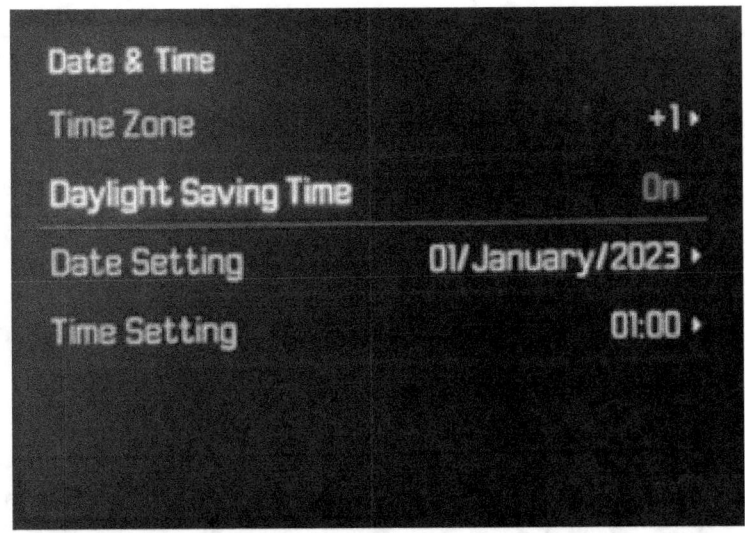

4. Pick either "On" or "Off."

Exploring External Camera Features

Topside controls

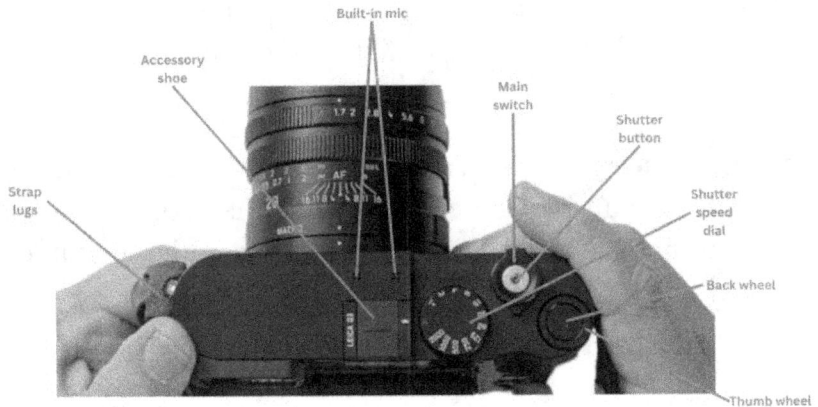

1. **Power Switch:** This lever turns the camera on and off. Simple as that!

2. **Strap Lugs:** These metal loops on the sides of the camera body allow you to attach a camera strap for carrying it comfortably around your neck or shoulder.

3. **Shutter Button:** This button takes the picture when you press it down all the way. A half-press helps the camera focus.

4. **Speed Dial:** This dial controls how long the shutter stays open, letting in more or less light. Think of it like a dimmer switch for your photos.

5. **Back Wheel:** This dial on the back lets you adjust things like the aperture (opening size for light), ISO (light sensitivity), or browse through menus. It's like a mini joystick for your camera settings.

6. **Wheel Button:** This button in the center of the back wheel confirms your choices or activates things you've set it to do in the menu. Think of it like an "Enter" key for your camera.

7. **Accessory Shoe:** This hot shoe mounted on the top plate expands your creative horizons. You can attach external flashes, microphones, or electronic viewfinders, enhancing the Q3's functionality for diverse shooting scenarios.

8. **Shoe Mount:** This little slot on top lets you attach extra things like flashes, microphones, or even a viewfinder if you want. It's like a plug-in for extra camera tools.

9. **Built-in Mic:** This tiny microphone picks up sound for your videos or adds background noise to your photos. It's like a built-in recorder for your camera.

10. **Timer Light:** This little light blinks when you're using the self-timer, counting down until the picture is taken. It's also a helpful light for focusing in the dark.

Front features

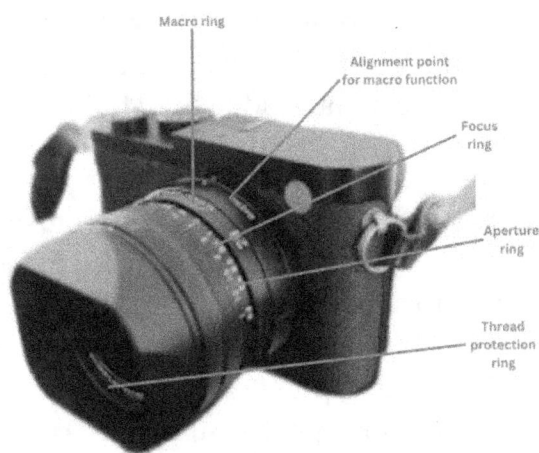

1. **HDMI Output:** This port, usually hidden behind a rubber flap, allows you to connect your Q3 to an external monitor or TV. This is handy for viewing your photos and videos on a larger screen, especially helpful for group viewing or when editing footage.

2. **USB-C Output:** This versatile port serves multiple purposes. Primarily, it's used for charging the Q3's battery using the provided cable. Additionally, it enables data transfer, allowing you to offload your captured photos and videos to a computer for editing or storage. Some external accessories like handgrips might also connect through this port for extended functionality.

3. **AF and MF Lock Release:** This small button located near the lens base plays a crucial role in focusing. In autofocus (AF) mode, pressing it locks the focus distance you've chosen, even if you recompose the frame. This is useful for maintaining focus on a specific subject while maneuvering the camera. If you switch to manual focus (MF) mode, this button temporarily disengages the lens focus mechanism, allowing you to rotate the focus ring freely for precise manual adjustments.

4. **Focus Tab:** This small, textured lever positioned near the lens base offers another way to control focusing. Pulling it towards you activates manual focus mode, allowing you to adjust the focus ring directly. Pushing it back towards the lens engages autofocus mode. This alternative focusing method provides a tactile and familiar feel for photographers accustomed to traditional film cameras.

5. **Macro Ring:** This ring around the lens base controls the focusing distance in macro mode, allowing you to achieve precise focus on small subjects.

6. **Focus Ring:** This ring on the lens barrel allows you to manually adjust the focus distance in manual focus mode.

7. **Aperture Ring:** This ring on the lens controls the aperture size, which determines the amount of light entering the camera and affects the depth of field in your photos.

8. **Thread Protection Ring:** This front-most ring on the lens protects the filter threads from scratches and dust when you're not using a filter.

9. **Microphone:** This built-in microphone captures the soundtrack to your visuals. It's ideal for recording ambient sounds or basic audio accompaniment for your videos.

10. **Self-Timer LED / AF Assist Lamp:** This tiny light serves two purposes. In self-timer mode, it blinks to indicate the remaining time

Back-of-the-body controls

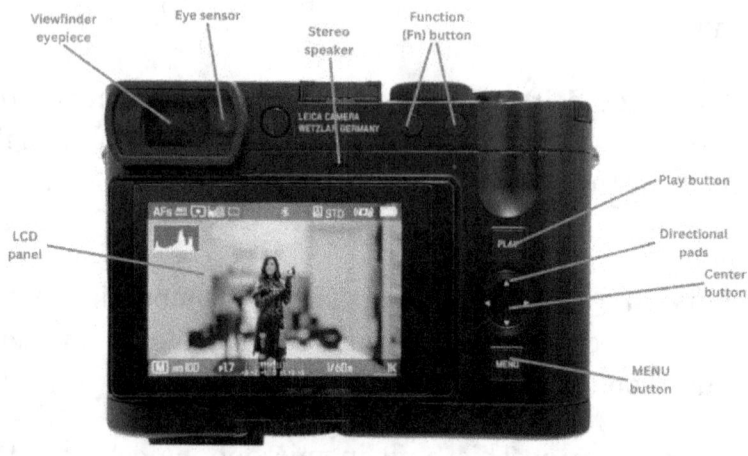

1. **LCD Panel:** This bright and high-resolution touchscreen display allows you to preview your shots, review captured images and videos, navigate the camera menu, and adjust various settings. It also tilts up and down for more comfortable viewing at low or high angles.

2. **Viewfinder Eyepiece:** Nestled on the top left corner, this electronic viewfinder (EVF) provides an alternative to the LCD screen for composing your shots, especially in bright sunlight. It offers high resolution and a clear view of the scene.

3. **Eye Sensor:** This sensor automatically detects when your eye approaches the viewfinder and turns it on, while switching off the LCD screen for a more immersive shooting experience.

4. **Diopter Wheel:** Located near the viewfinder eyepiece, this wheel allows you to adjust the focus of the eyepiece for optimal viewing if you wear glasses.

5. **Function (FN) Buttons:** Two customizable buttons located on the right side of the LCD screen let you assign frequently used functions for quick access. You can choose from various options like exposure lock, white balance, focus peaking, or bracketing.

6. **Menu Button:** This button grants access to the camera's main menu, where you can explore and adjust various settings like image quality, autofocus mode, metering options, and video recording parameters.

7. **Directional Pad:** This four-way joystick helps you navigate through the menu options, adjust settings, and select specific points on the LCD screen.

8. **Play Button:** Located below the directional pad, this button initiates playback of captured videos and allows you to review photos in single-image or continuous playback mode.

9. **Center Button:** This multi-functional button confirms selections in the menu or acts as an "Enter" key when navigating settings. It also serves as the "OK" button for confirming actions like deleting photos.

10. **Status LED:** This small light on the back panel indicates the camera's current state, such as when it's saving images, recording video, or connected to Wi-Fi.

11. **Stereo Speaker:** This built-in speaker allows you to playback the audio recorded alongside your videos directly on the camera.

12. **Alignment Point for Macro Function:** This small dot on the back of the camera aligns with a corresponding mark on the lens to activate the macro focus mode, ideal for capturing close-up shots.

Working with Memory Cards

Memory cards already used with this camera will usually not require formatting. If you put a new memory card into the camera for the first time, you need to format it before using it. We recommend occasionally formatting memory cards because residual data traces (data about individual shots) may reduce memory capacity.

➤ Select Format Card in the main menu.

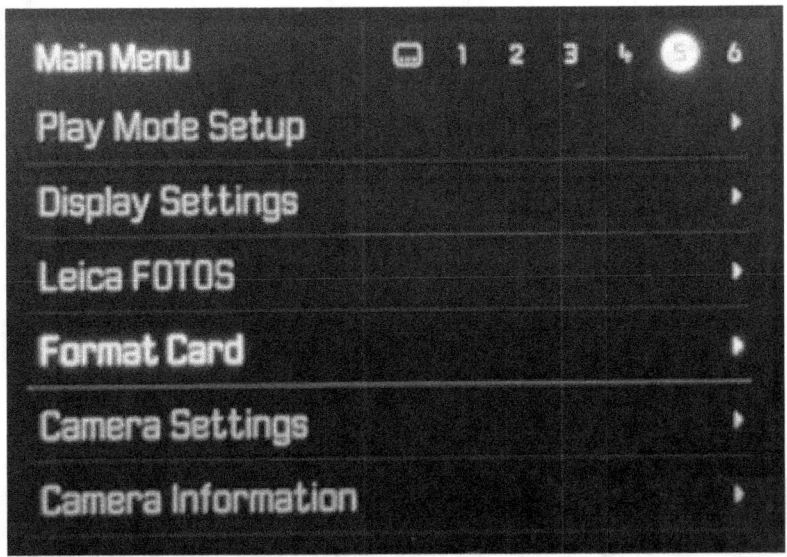

> Confirm the selection.

   o   The status LED will flash during the process.

Remember:

1. Don't turn off the camera while moving pictures or videos.

2. When you format the memory card, everything on it will be deleted. It won't stop formatting even if you have protection on some shots.

3. Move your photos to a safe place, like your computer, regularly.

4. Simple formatting won't completely erase your data, just the directory. You can recover it with the right software, except for the data overwritten by new stuff.

5. If you format the memory card in a different device, like a computer, format it again in the camera.

CHAPTER 2: FOCUSING

Your Leica Q3 camera can focus on its own or with manual control. It has three modes and four metering methods for autofocus photography.

AF Photography

Autofocus (AF) in photography refers to the camera's ability to automatically adjust its focus to ensure that the subject appears sharp and clear in the captured image. In the context of the Leica Q3, the autofocus system plays a crucial role in achieving precise and quick focusing. Here are key aspects related to AF photography in the Leica Q3:

- **Autofocus System:** The Leica Q3 is equipped with an autofocus system that facilitates automatic focusing, relieving the photographer from the manual adjustment of focus. This is particularly useful in situations where the subject is moving or when quick and accurate focusing is essential.

- **Hybrid Autofocus System:** The Leica Q3 may feature a hybrid autofocus system, combining different autofocus technologies for enhanced performance. Hybrid systems often include phase detection, contrast detection, and depth-from-defocus (DFD) technologies to optimize focusing speed and accuracy.

- **Phase Detection Autofocus:** Phase detection is a technology that allows the camera to measure the convergence of two beams of light, ensuring faster autofocus acquisition. This is especially beneficial when capturing moving subjects or shooting in challenging lighting conditions.

- **Contrast Detection Autofocus:** Contrast detection analyzes the contrast in the scene to determine the point of focus. While it may not be as fast as phase detection, contrast detection is often more accurate, particularly in low-contrast scenes.

- **Subject Recognition:** Intelligent subject recognition is likely incorporated into the autofocus system of the Leica Q3. This feature helps identify and track subjects such as people, animals, or specific objects, enhancing the camera's ability to maintain focus on the intended subject.

- **5.76 MP OLED Viewfinder:** The Leica Q3 is equipped with a 5.76 MP OLED viewfinder, providing a high-resolution and clear display for composing images and confirming focus. The viewfinder ensures that photographers can confidently assess the focus and composition before capturing the shot.

- **Quick and Accurate Focusing:** The autofocus system in the Leica Q3 is designed to deliver quick and accurate focusing, enabling photographers to capture spontaneous moments and ensuring that the resulting images are sharp and well-focused.

Here's how you can set your Q3 to AF:

1. Press and keep holding the AF/MF release button.

2. Turn the focus ring to the AF position.

3. Adjust the AF frame to the desired position.

4. Tap and hold the shutter button.

   - Focusing happens once (AFs) or continuously (AFc).

   - Successful metering: AF frame turns green.

   - Unsuccessful metering: AF frame turns red.

   - Alternatively, configure and save focus/exposure settings using a function button like the shutter release.

MF Photography

Manual Focus (MF) photography refers to the process of manually adjusting the focus of the camera lens rather than relying on automatic focusing systems. In the Leica Q3, manual focus provides photographers with precise control over the focus point, allowing for creative expression and accuracy in capturing images. Here are key aspects related to MF photography in the Leica Q3:

- **Manual Focus Ring:** The Leica Q3 is equipped with a manual focus ring that allows users to manually adjust the focus of the lens. The focus ring is typically located around the lens barrel and provides a tactile and direct way for photographers to control the focus.

- **Focus Magnification:** To aid in manual focusing, the Leica Q3 may feature a focus magnification function. This allows photographers to zoom in on a portion of the image in the viewfinder or display, making it easier to fine-tune the focus for precise results.

- **Manual Focus Assist Tools:** The camera may offer additional manual focus assist tools, such as distance scales or depth-of-field indicators, to help photographers gauge the focus distance and make informed adjustments.

- **Hybrid Autofocus with Manual Override:** In some situations, photographers may prefer to start with autofocus and then fine-tune the focus manually. The Leica Q3 may offer a hybrid autofocus system that allows for manual override, providing flexibility in the focusing process.

- **Precision and Creative Control:** Manual focusing in the Leica Q3 provides photographers with precise control over the focus point, allowing them to emphasize specific elements in the frame or achieve a desired aesthetic. This level of control is particularly valuable in situations where autofocus may struggle, such as low-light conditions or scenes with low contrast.

- **Use in Challenging Conditions:** Manual focus is often favored in challenging shooting conditions where autofocus may be less reliable. Photographers can take advantage of manual focus when capturing macro shots, shooting through obstacles, or working in situations with rapidly changing scenes.

Here's how you can set your Q3 to MF:

1. Keep the AF/MF release button pressed.

2. Rotate the focus ring in a direction opposite to the AF position.

3. Adjust the focus ring to manually focus on the object.

4. Press the shutter release button.

Autofocus Modes

You can choose how your camera focuses with different modes: AFs, AFc, and Intelligent AF. The default setting is Intelligent AF. To change it, go to the main menu, select Focusing, and choose your preferred setting (Intelligent AF, AFs, or AFc). The selected mode will be displayed in the header line.

Intelligent AF

Works for everything. The camera picks either AFs or AFc on its own.

Focusing	
Focus Mode	Intelligent AF ▸
AF Mode	[⋅⋅⋅] ▸
AF Assist Lamp	On
Focus Assist	▸
Touch AF	Touch AF ▸
Touch AF in EVF	▸

AFs (single)

The Leica Q3's AFs (single) mode shines for capturing still life and meticulously staged scenes. This focus mode takes precision aiming to heart. By half-pressing the shutter button, you lock focus on your chosen subject, even if you recompose the frame or briefly turn the camera away. This is like "tagging" your target with focus, allowing you to maneuver confidently without disturbing the critical sharpness. Think of it as setting the focal point on a beautiful still life arrangement or pinpointing a captivating detail on a majestic landscape – this mode ensures unwavering sharpness while you refine your composition.

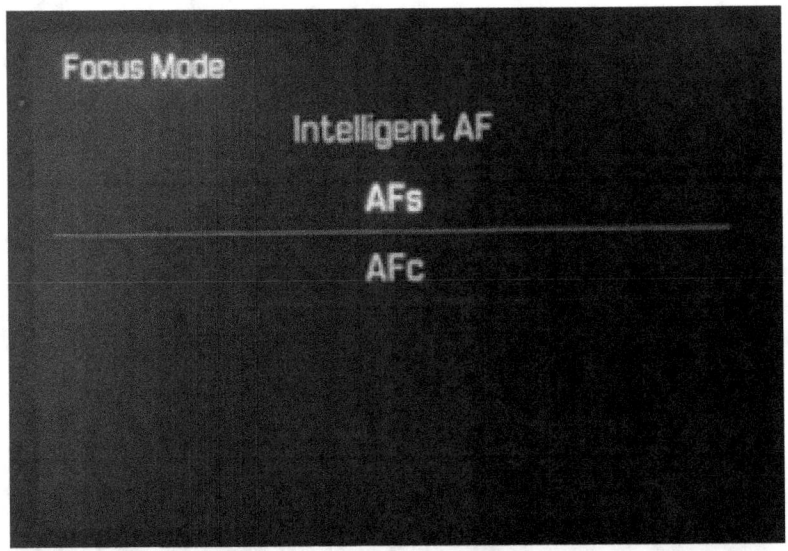

However, for dynamic subjects or fast-paced action, AFs (single) might not be the ideal choice. Since focus remains locked until you half-press the shutter again, capturing a fleeting expression or a mid-stride moment might elude the camera's grasp. For such situations, consider exploring other autofocus modes on the Q3, like AFc (continuous) for tracking movement, or AFi (intelligent) for automatically adapting to various scenarios.

AFC (continuous)

AFC (continuous) is like having a built-in assistant for your camera, especially when things are on the move. When you press the shutter button halfway, the camera keeps adjusting the focus to stay locked on your subject, even if they're walking, running, or just fidgeting. Think of it like a spotlight that follows your subject around, making sure they're always crystal clear in the picture.

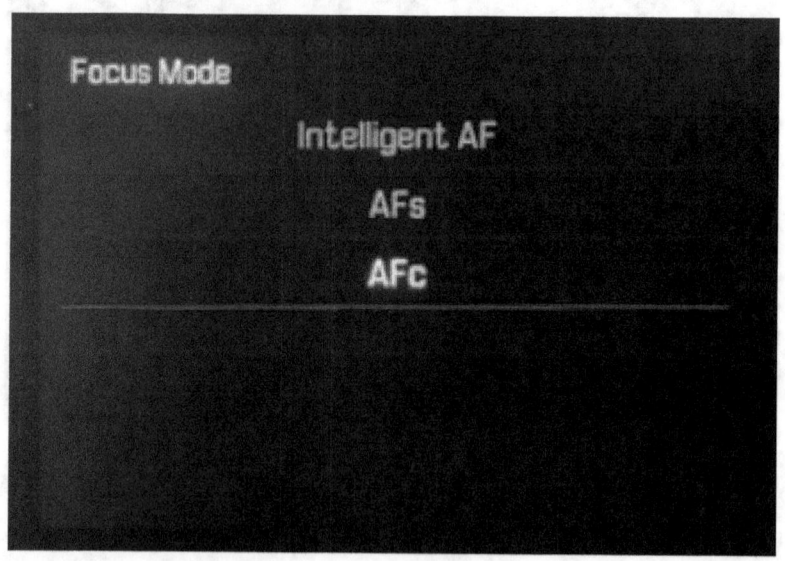

This is great for capturing kids playing, pets running around, or athletes in action. You don't have to worry about constantly refocusing, just aim and shoot, and the camera does the rest.

However, AFC isn't perfect. Sometimes, if your subject moves out of the center of the frame, the camera might focus on something else for a moment before catching up. So, it's better for capturing the overall movement rather than specific details.

Autofocus Metering Methods

The AF mode helps you focus on different methods. A successful focus is shown in green, and an unsuccessful one is red.

To change settings:

1. Go to the main menu and select "Focusing."

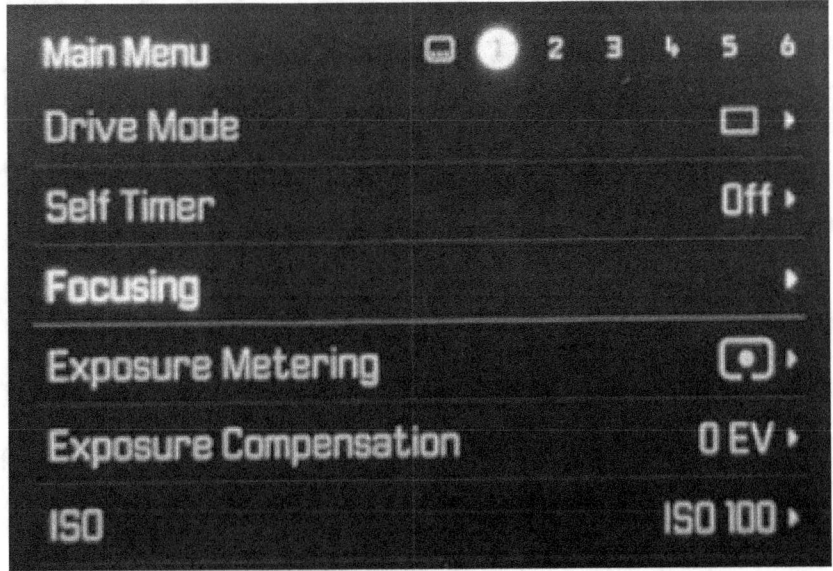

2. Choose "AF Mode."

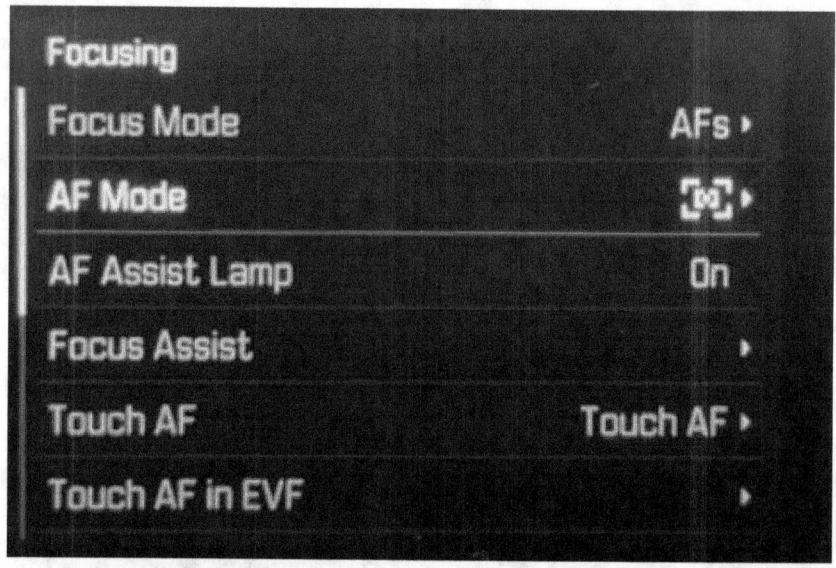

3. Pick the setting you want, like Multi-Field, Spot, Field, Zone, Tracking, Eye/Face/Body Detection, or Eye/Face/Body + Animal Detection.

Notes

➢ Auto-focus might not work well:

○ When the object is too far or too close.

➢ if the object isn't well-lit

• Touch auto-focus lets you put the focus frame directly where you want.

Multi-field Metering

Multi-field metering tells your camera how much light to let in. Instead of focusing on just one part of the picture, it takes a quick look at the whole scene – the bright sky, the dark trees, your smiling face – and figures out the best amount of light for everything to look good.

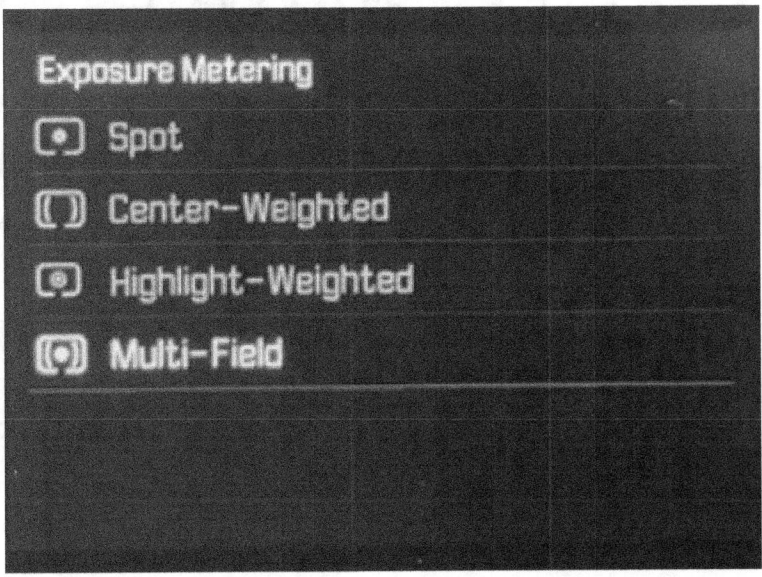

This is great for taking quick pictures when you don't have time to mess with settings. Just point and shoot, and Multi-field makes sure your photos aren't too dark or too bright. It's like having a built-in cheat code for perfect exposure!

Spot/field Metering

Both ways only see the object parts inside specific frames. These frames look like a small box (field metering) or a cross (spot metering). Spot metering is good for focusing on small details, while field metering is less picky but still allows selective metering. You can use these methods for taking multiple shots with the focused part always in the same spot – just move the frame to a different position.

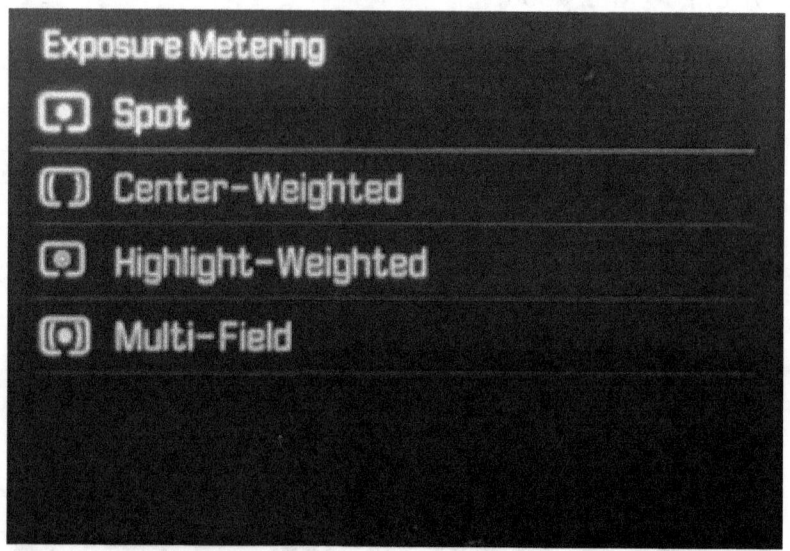

Zone

This metering method organizes subject sections into a clear 5x5 group. It provides security for snapshots and the ability to reliably focus on larger objects. After setting it up, focus frames appear to highlight the object's focused areas.

Tracking

This special camera setting helps capture things that are moving. It keeps adjusting the focus on whatever is in the focus frame. Here's how to use it:

- Point the focus frame at what you want.

- Move the camera if needed.

- Tap and hold the shutter button.

or

➢ If you press the function button set to AF-L or AF-L + AE-L, the camera will focus on the object.

➢ Move the camera to the part you want in the shot.

  ○ The focus frame follows the chosen object, adjusting focus continuously.

This metering method always adjusts focus, even when the AF mode is set to AFs.

Person Detection (Face Detection)

Person detection means the camera recognizes faces and detects the body, helping it stay focused on a person even if their face isn't visible. It prevents the camera from randomly switching to other faces in the frame. When the camera detects eyes, it focuses on them, and you can choose which eye or face to focus on using the directional pad. The selected eye or face will be highlighted.

Eye/Face/Body + Animal Detection

With a focus on precision and versatility, the Eye/Face/Body + Animal Detection feature takes a significant leap forward. This innovative update not only refines the camera's ability to detect and focus on human eyes, faces, and bodies but also extends its recognition prowess to include common pets.

Users can experience a heightened level of convenience and accuracy when capturing moments that involve animals. Whether it's your beloved dog, cat, or other domestic companions, the Leica Q3's advanced detection system ensures that your camera can intelligently identify and track these subjects. This expansion in functionality opens up new creative possibilities, allowing photographers to effortlessly capture candid and engaging shots of both people and their furry friends.

AF Quick Setting

The AF Quick Setting typically refers to a feature that allows users to quickly access and adjust autofocus settings on their camera for efficient and convenient operation. It lets you easily change the focus frame size in certain autofocus modes. The screen image stays visible while you make adjustments.

Accessing AF Quick Setting

- ➤ Press and keep your finger on the screen.

  - ○ Extra screens disappear.

  - ○ • Red triangles appear at two corners of the focus frame when using specific metering methods like Field, Zone, Eye/Face, Body Detection, or Eye/Face/Body + Animal Detection.

Adjusting the AF Frame Size

Adjust the autofocus frame size by turning the thumbwheel or using a two-finger pinch/spread, with three size options available.

Enlargement in AF Mode

Using the enlargement function, you can zoom in to check settings without focusing. Just assign the Magnification function to a function button to enable this feature.

Assigning a function to a function button

You can quickly access menu functions while taking photos by assigning them to these buttons: FN button 1, FN button 2, Center button, and Thumbwheel button. The assignments for photo and video mode are separate.

Submenus might look different when you access them directly than access through the main menu. They often show up as menu bars for easy settings. Depending on the submenu type, you can adjust settings using keys or touch control on the LCD panel.

Changing an assignment:

➤ Choose the mode you want (photo or video).

➤ Hold down the function button.

- Your custom shortcuts will show up on the screen.

- You can change these shortcuts anytime in the Customize Control menu.

➤ Pick the option you want by pressing the center button.

- No need to confirm – the change happens right away.

Accessing the enlargement function

➤ Press the function button.

- A bigger picture part shows up. Where it shows up depends on where the AF frame is.

- The rectangle in the frame's top right shows how much we've zoomed in and where that zoomed-in part is on the screen.

Adjusting the enlargement function

➤ Tap the middle button

- The picture area switches between zoom levels.

Changing the position of the enlarged section

Push the arrow buttons in the right direction.

Exiting the enlargement function

➤ Touch the button to take a photo

or

➤ Push the function button once more

Remember, the zoom keeps working until you close it. The last zoom level you used will stay when you open it again.

Manual Focusing (MF)

Sometimes, focusing your camera manually is better than relying on autofocus. This is true when you're using the same camera settings for multiple shots, need to keep the focus at infinity for landscapes, or if it's too dark for autofocus to work well. To manually focus, move the focus ring away from the autofocus position and turn it until your subject looks sharp.

MF Assist Functions

Manual Focus (MF) Assist Functions are features designed to aid photographers when manually focusing their lenses. These functions enhance the precision and ease of manual focusing, especially in situations where achieving critical focus is crucial. In MF mode, you can use these helper functions.

Focus Peaking

This tool helps you highlight the edges of the focused parts in a picture using color. You can choose the color and adjust the sensitivity.

1. Go to the main menu and select "Focusing."

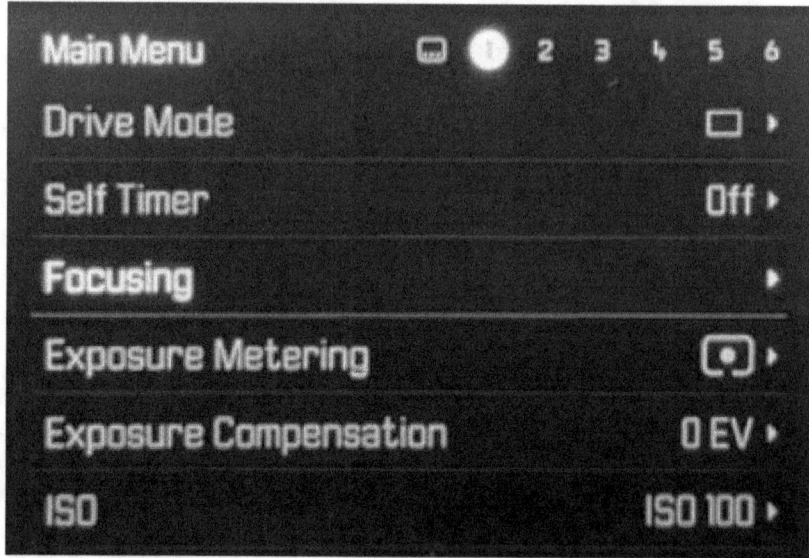

2. Choose "Focus Assist."

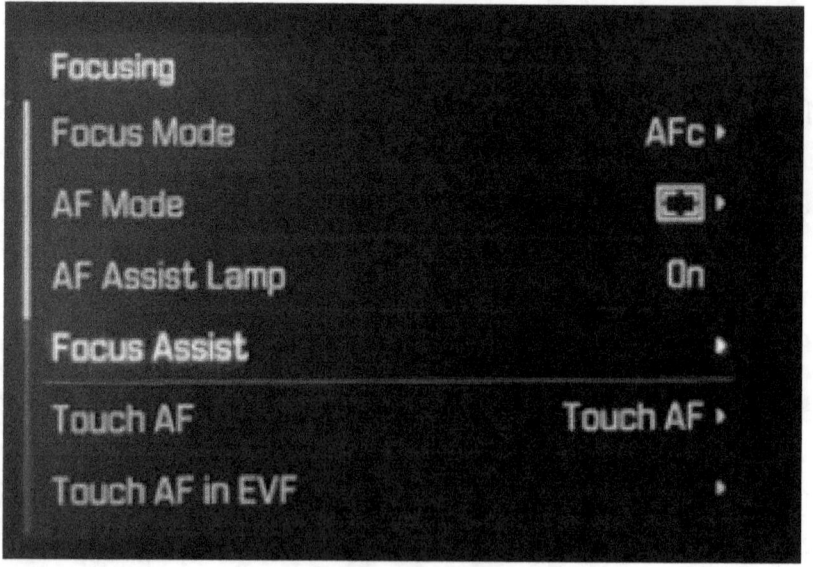

3. Select "Focus Peaking."

4. Pick a setting: Off, Red, Green, Blue, or White.

5. Choose a part of the image.

6. Turn the focus ring to highlight the subject you want.

Focus peaking highlights areas with a lot of contrast, like the difference between light and dark. So, even if something isn't perfectly in focus, it might still be marked if it has high contrast.

Enlargement in MF Mode

Seeing more details of an object helps you judge how clear it is and lets you focus more accurately. This feature can turn on by itself when you manually focus or be used separately.

Access Via the Focus Ring

Twist the focus ring to make part of the picture bigger. Here's how:

1. Go to the main menu and choose "Focusing."

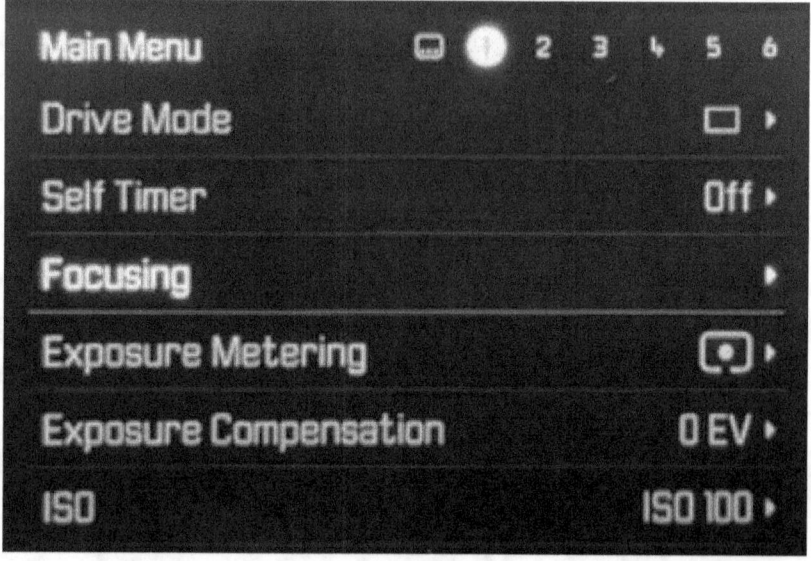

2. Pick "Focus Assist."

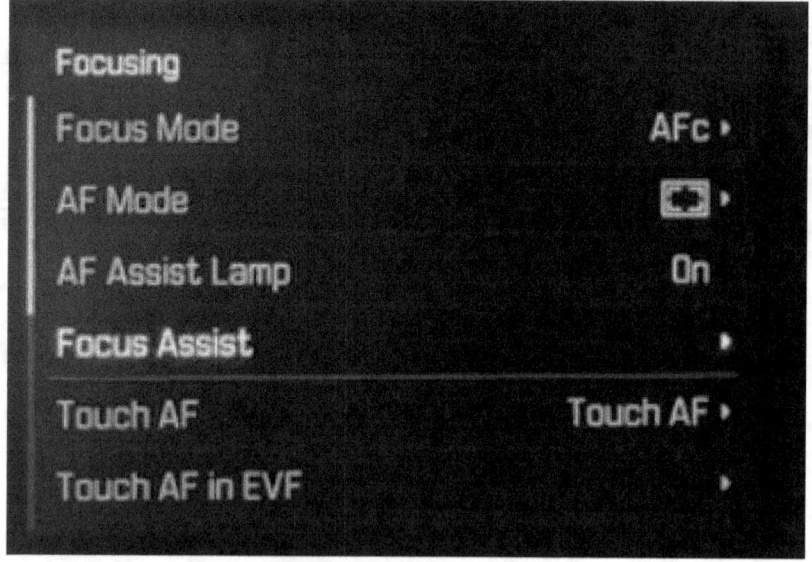

3. Choose "Auto Magnification."

4. Set it to "On."

5. Turn the focus ring.

You'll see a larger part of the image, and its position depends on where the AF frame is. The rectangle in the top right shows the magnification and its place in the cropped section.

Adjusting the enlargement function

Press the middle button to switch between zoom levels in the image section.

Changing the position of the enlarged section

Push the arrow buttons in the right direction.

Exiting the enlargement function

Press the button to take a picture.

The zoom will return to its regular size after not being adjusted for about 5 seconds. Your last zoom level will stay when you use the feature again.

Access Via the Function Button

You can zoom in separately from focusing to get a clearer look at settings. Just assign the Magnification function to one of the buttons to use this feature.

Assigning a function to a function button

You can choose certain functions for quick access in shooting mode by assigning them to these buttons: FN button 1, FN button 2, Center button, and Thumbwheel button. What you set for photo mode won't affect video mode, and vice versa.

Going directly to submenus might look different than when you access them through the main menu. Usually, they show up as menu bars for easy adjustments. You can change settings by pressing keys or using touch controls on the screen; the mode depends on the submenu type.

Changing an assignment

1. Choose whether you want to take a photo or record a video.

2. Hold down the function button.

3. The options you've set will show up on the screen.

4. You can change these options anytime in the "Customize Control" menu.

5. Pick the option you want by pressing the center button.

6. Your choice is applied right away without needing confirmation.

Accessing the enlargement function

1. Press the function button.

2. A bigger part of the picture shows up. Where it shows depends on where the AF frame is.

3. The rectangle in the top right corner shows how much it's zoomed in and where that part is in the picture.

Adjusting the enlargement function

Press the middle button to zoom in or out on the image. Swipe to change the position of the zoomed-in area.

or

Press the arrow buttons in the right direction.

Exiting the enlargement function

Press the button to take a picture.

Note: The making things bigger feature stays on until you turn it off.

CHAPTER 3: CHOOSING BASIC PICTURE SETTINGS

Selecting an Exposure Mode

You can choose from four modes to control how your pictures look:

- Program mode (P)

- Aperture mode (A)

- Shutter mode (S)

- Manual mode (M)

To use the basic modes (P, A, S, M) on your camera, make sure you first set the Scene Mode correctly. Choose the P-A-S-M option in the menu. If you pick one of the ten automatic program modes, it will override the manual settings on the shutter-speed dial and aperture ring.

The four operating modes turn on by themselves when you use specific settings together.

	Setting via the shutter-speed dial	Setting via the aperture ring
P	A	A

A	A	Manual setting (not A)
S	Manual setting (not A)	A
M	Manual setting (not A)	Manual setting (not A)

Choose "Scene Mode" from the main menu, then select "P-A-S-M." Adjust the shutter-speed dial and aperture ring to the right settings.

Fully Automatic Exposure Setting – P

Program AE Mode – P

Use AE mode for quick and automatic photos. Follow these steps:

1. Choose "Scene Mode" from the main menu.

2. Select "P-A-S-M."

3. Set the shutter speed dial and aperture ring to the A position.

4. Hold down the shutter button.

   - Exposure info appears at the bottom, showing auto-set aperture and shutter speed.

   - Other info bars will be hidden.

5. Take the photo by releasing the shutter button.

6. Optionally, adjust the auto-set values (Program shift).

Changing the Preset Shutter Speed and Aperture Combinations (Shift)

Adjusting the preset settings using the Shift function lets you control the exposure speed and aperture while keeping the overall image brightness constant. You can choose faster shutter speeds for sports photos and slower speeds for more depth in landscape shots. Turn the thumbwheel right for greater depth of field or left for faster shutter speeds. Shifted values are marked with an asterisk next to the P.

Make sure to adjust within the specified range to get the right exposure.

Semi-Automatic Exposure Setting – A/S

Aperture-Priority Mode - A

In Aperture-priority mode, the camera automatically adjusts the exposure based on your chosen aperture. It is great for photos where the depth of field matters a lot. Pick a low aperture for a focused face with a blurry background in portraits, or go for a higher aperture to have everything in focus from the front to the back in landscape photos.

1. Go to the main menu and choose "Scene Mode."

2. Select "P-A-S-M" from the options.

3. Rotate the shutter speed dial to the A (Automatic) position.

4. Pick your preferred aperture value.

5. Press and hold the shutter button.

6. Look at the bottom of the screen for exposure info, showing the automatically set aperture and shutter speed. Other info bars will be hidden.

7. Finally, release the shutter to take a photo.

Shutter-Priority Mode - S

When you use shutter-priority mode, you pick how fast the camera shutter opens and closes, and the camera figures out the rest for the correct exposure. This mode works well for capturing moving things; a quick shutter speed stops motion for clear shots, while a slower one adds a sense of motion with cool effects.

1. Go to the main menu and choose "Scene Mode."

2. Select "P-A-S-M."

3. Turn the aperture ring to the "A" position.

4. Pick your preferred shutter speed:

   - Use the shutter speed dial for full increments.

   - Use the thumbwheel for fine-tuning in 1/3 increments.

5. Press and hold the shutter button:

   - Exposure info appears at the bottom screen, showing the automatically set aperture and shutter speed.

   - Other info bars will be hidden.

6. Release the shutter button to take the photo.

You can also adjust settings on the status screen instead of using fine-tuning. Depending on the thumbwheel assignment, it might be the only choice.

Manual Setting Setting - M

Choose specific shutter speed and aperture settings:

- To give your photo a unique atmosphere from a specific exposure type.

- For consistent exposure across multiple images with different crops.

Here's how:

1. Go to Scene Mode in the main menu.

2. Choose P-A-S-M.

3. Set the exposure manually using the shutter-speed dial and aperture ring.

- Adjust exposure compensation using the light balance scale.

4. Hold the shutter button to see exposure info at the bottom of the screen.

    - Other info bars will be hidden.

5. Finally, press the shutter button to capture your photo.

When you choose P-A-S-M in the Exposure Preview menu, the screen will display an exposure preview after metering. Set the shutter speed to one of the marked values on the dial.

Choosing a Drive Mode

The Leica Q3 has different ways to take pictures, and this usually talks about how each photo is taken. Besides taking one picture at a time, there are other ways to do it.

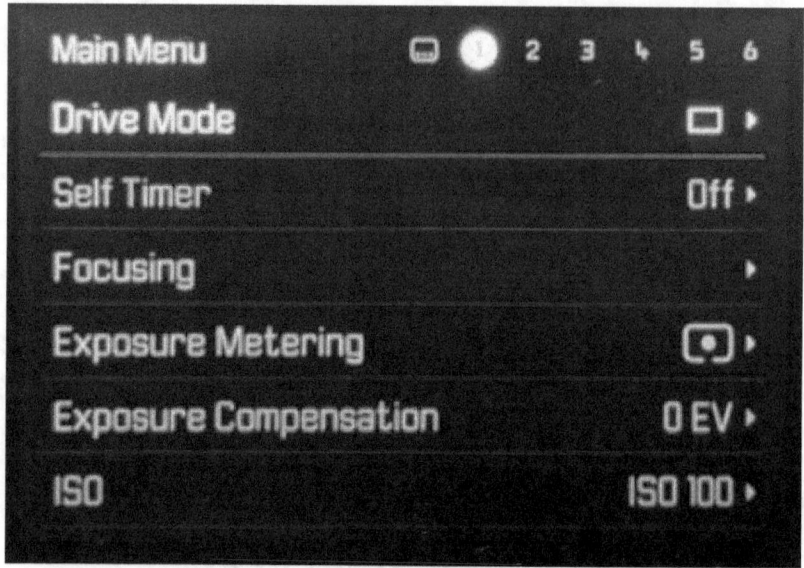

To learn more about these ways and options, go to the main menu and choose "Drive Mode." Then, pick the function you want.

Drive mode	Setting options/ Variants
Single frame shooting	Single

Continuous shooting	Speed:
	
	  – Continuous - 2 fps / 14 bit / AF
	
	  – Continuous - 4 fps / 14 bit / AF
	
	  – Continuous - 7 fps / 14 bit

	– Continuous - 9 fps / 12 bit – Continuous - 15 fps / 12 bit
Interval shooting	Number of Frames Interval between the shootings (Interval) Delay time (Countdown)
Exposure bracketing	Number of Frames (3 or 5) EV Steps Exposure Compensation Automatic
Self-timer	Delay time: – Self-timer 2 s – Self-timer 12 s

Single frame shooting

Single frame shooting in the Leica Q3 refers to a shooting mode where the camera captures individual images with each press of the shutter release button. This mode is ideal for situations where you want precise control over each shot, allowing you to carefully compose and time your photographs.

Drive Mode
- ☐ Single
- Continuous – 2 fps / 14 bit / AF
- Continuous – 4 fps / 14 bit / AF
- Continuous – 7 fps / 14 bit
- Continuous – 9 fps / 12 bit
- Continuous – 15 fps / 12 bit

In Single frame shooting mode, when you press the shutter release button, the camera takes a single exposure, making it suitable for capturing static subjects, portraits, or scenes where you want to ensure you get the perfect moment. This mode contrasts with continuous shooting modes, where the camera captures a series of images in rapid succession as long as the shutter button is held down.

Using Single frame shooting provides photographers with the ability to focus on the composition of each shot and make deliberate decisions before taking the next photo. It is often chosen for still photography, landscapes, or situations where you want to be more intentional and contemplative in your image-making process.

Continuous shooting

Continuous shooting, also known as burst mode, in the Leica Q3 is a shooting mode that allows the camera to capture a rapid sequence of images when the shutter release button is held down. This feature is particularly useful in situations where you need to capture fast-paced action or a series of moments in quick succession.

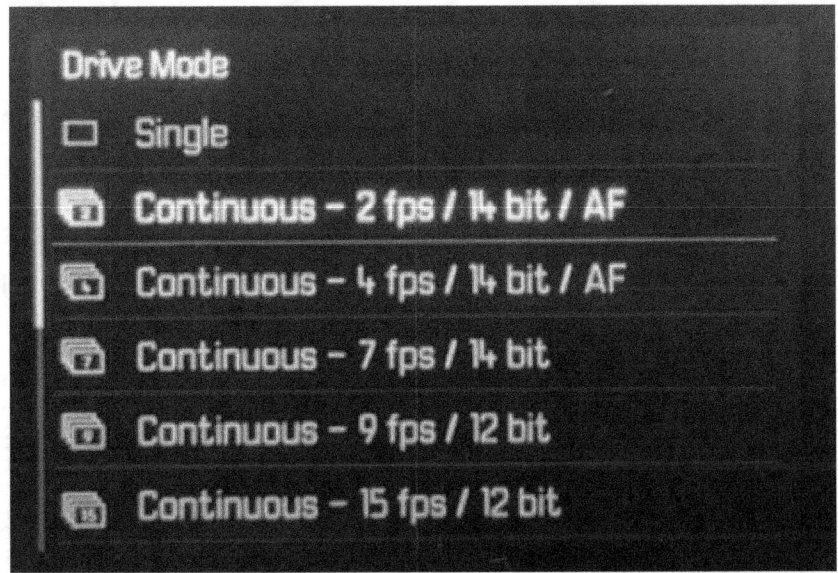

In Continuous shooting mode, the Leica Q3 will keep taking pictures as long as the shutter button is pressed and held. This mode is beneficial for various scenarios, such as sports photography, wildlife photography, or any situation where you want to ensure you don't miss a critical moment.

To engage Continuous shooting on the Leica Q3, you typically need to select this mode from the camera settings or mode dial.

The specific steps may vary depending on the camera's design, so it's advisable to refer to the camera's user manual for precise instructions.

To take multiple pictures in a row with your camera, follow these steps:

1. Go to the main menu and find "Drive Mode."

2. Choose the shooting you want:

    - Continuous at 2 frames per second with autofocus

    - Continuous at 4 frames per second with autofocus

    - Continuous at 7 frames per second without autofocus

    - Continuous at 9 frames per second with 12-bit quality

    - Continuous at 15 frames per second with 12-bit quality

Once you've selected it, the camera will take pictures continuously as long as you hold down the shutter button and have enough space on your memory card.

Tips:

1. Turn off preview mode (Auto Review) for better performance.

2. The last photo taken or saved during the saving process shows up first in both review modes, no matter how many shots were taken.

3. You can't do continuous shooting with a flash; it's single-shot only when the flash is on.

4. Continuous shooting mode can't be used with the self-timer.

5. The camera's buffer memory has limits, affecting the number of consecutive shots and the chosen exposure frequency. Once it's full, the speed slows down as data is transferred to the card, and the remaining shots are shown at the bottom right.

6. For shooting continuously at +2fps to +4fps, each shot gets its automatic settings like exposure, white balance, and autofocus.

7. If you're shooting rapidly at +7fps to +15fps, the automatic settings are applied to the first shot, and then the same settings are used for the rest of the shots in that series.

Interval shooting

The interval shooting feature on this camera introduces a powerful tool for capturing images automatically over an extended period, granting photographers the flexibility to document dynamic processes, changing scenes, or time-lapse sequences. In this mode, users have the autonomy to determine the number of shots, the time intervals between them, and precisely when the sequence begins.

By utilizing interval shooting, photographers can craft captivating visual narratives that unfold gradually over time. Whether it's capturing the progression of a sunset, the blossoming of a flower, or the movement of clouds in the sky, this feature empowers users to create compelling time-lapse sequences with ease.

However, it's crucial to be mindful of potential changes in lighting conditions and focus during the interval shooting process. Since the camera operates automatically over an extended duration, factors such as shifting sunlight or alterations in the subject's distance may impact the overall image quality. To mitigate these challenges, it's recommended to carefully plan the shooting parameters, consider the potential environmental changes, and make necessary adjustments to maintain consistent lighting and focus throughout the sequence.

Specifying the Number of Frames

1. Choose "Drive Mode" from the main menu.

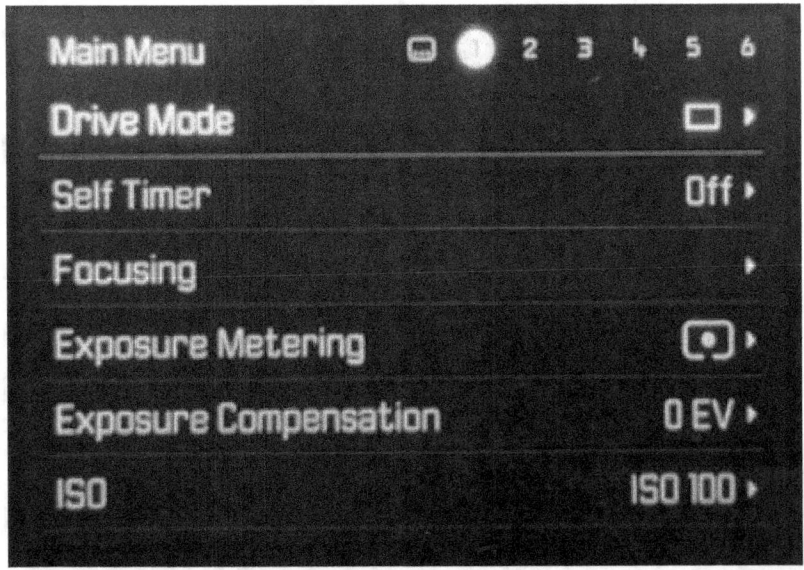

2. Pick "Interval Shooting."

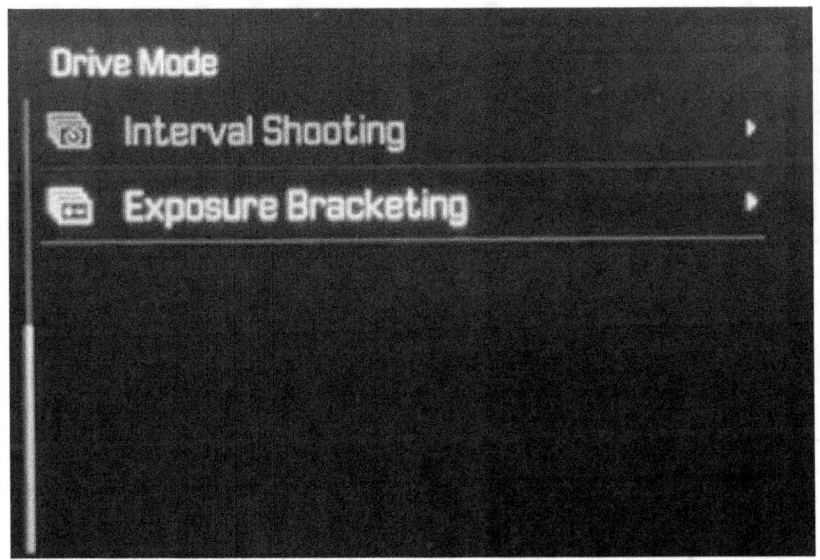

3. Select "Number of Frames."

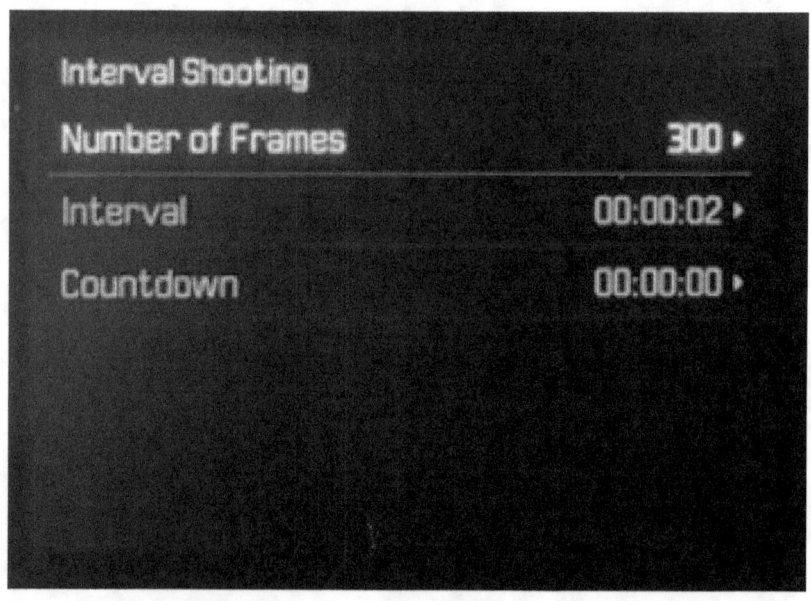

4. Enter the number you want.

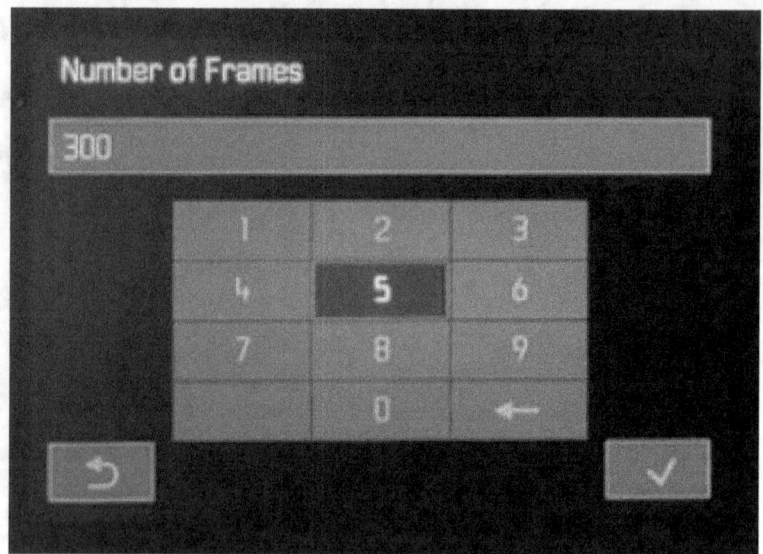

Specifying the Intervals Between Shots

1. Choose "Drive Mode" from the main menu.

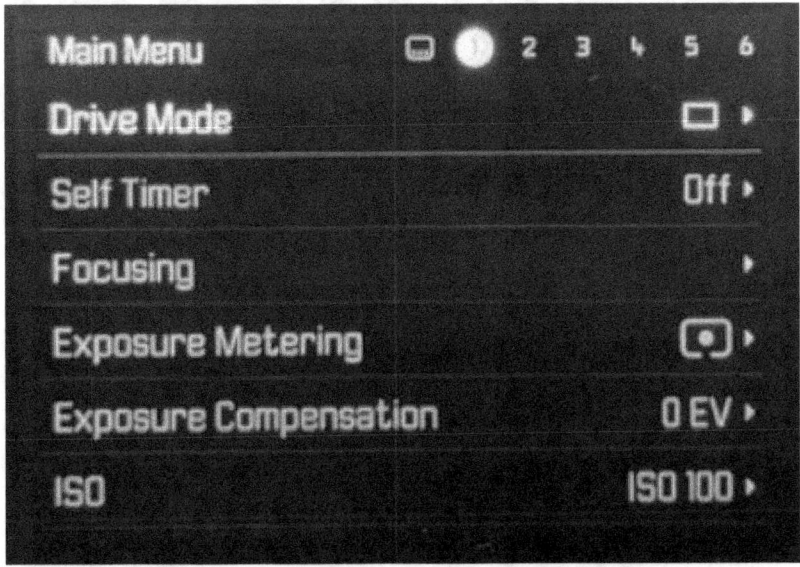

2. Then pick "Interval Shooting."

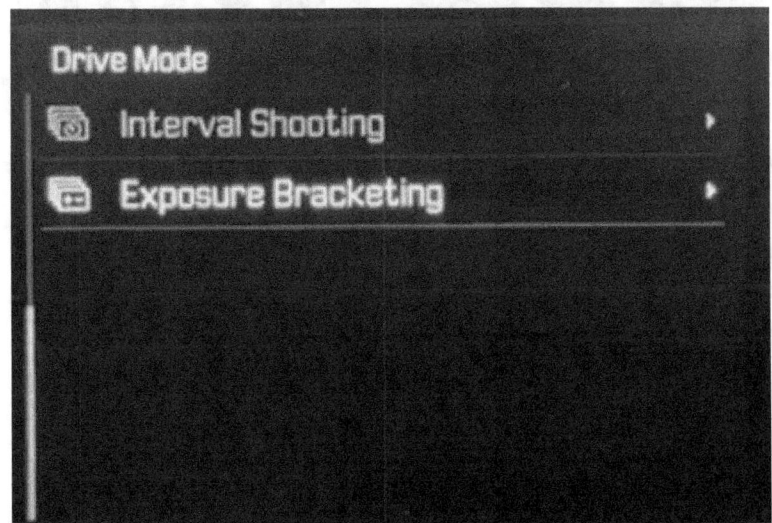

3. After that, select "Interval" and enter the value you want.

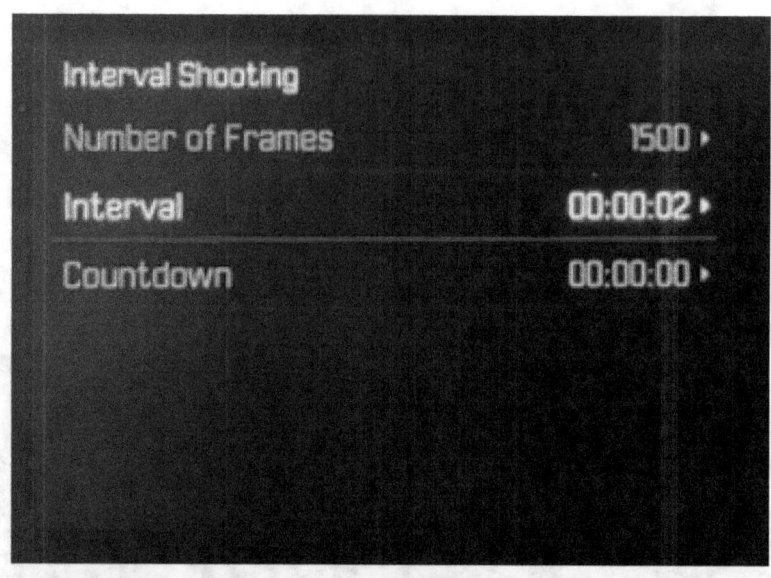

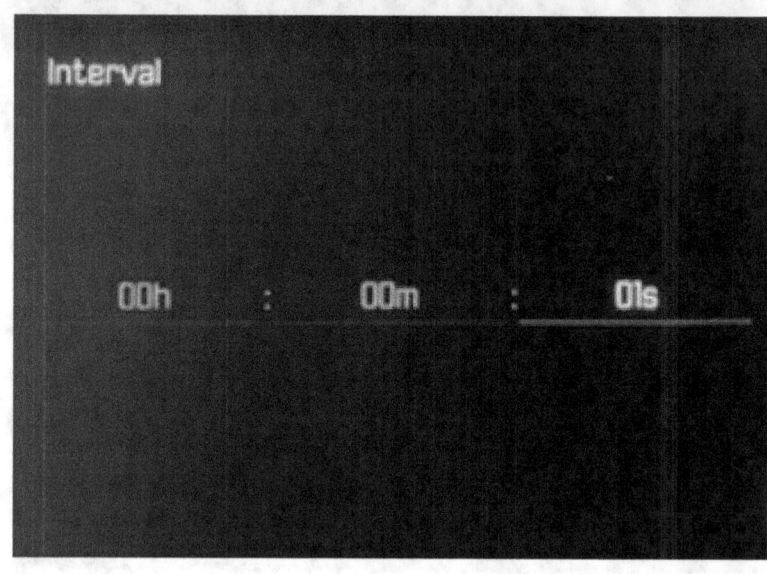

Setting the Delay Time

1. Choose "Drive Mode" from the main menu.

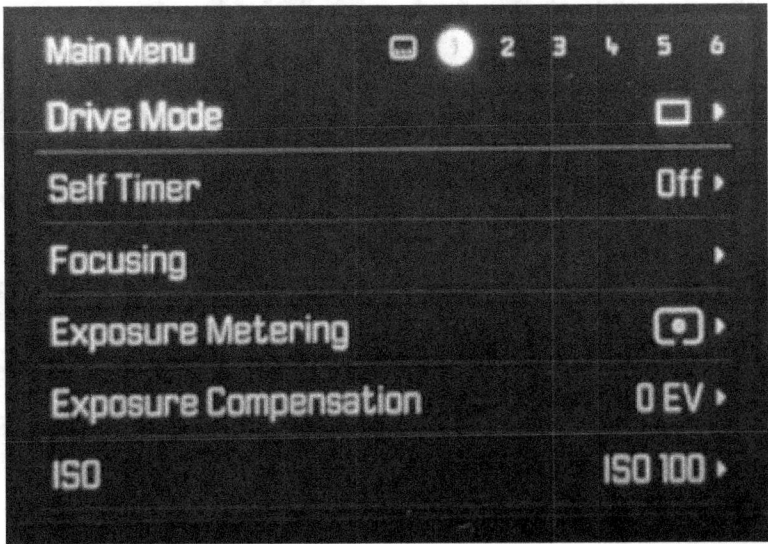

2. Then pick "Interval Shooting."

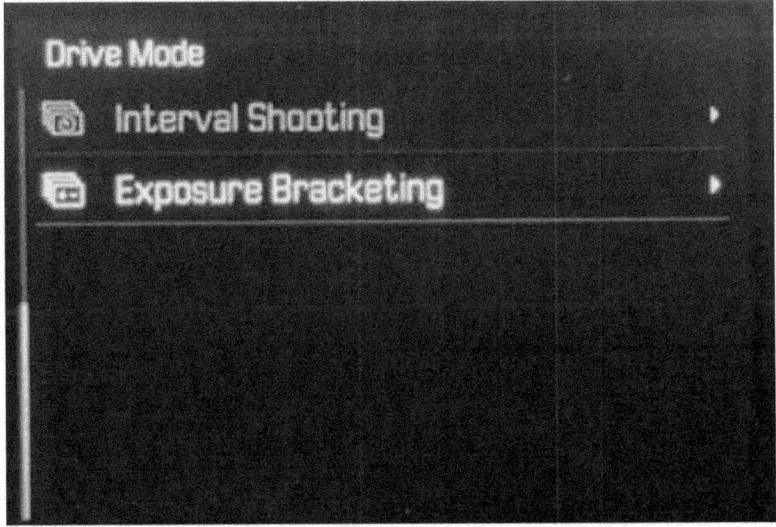

3. Select "Countdown," and enter your preferred value.

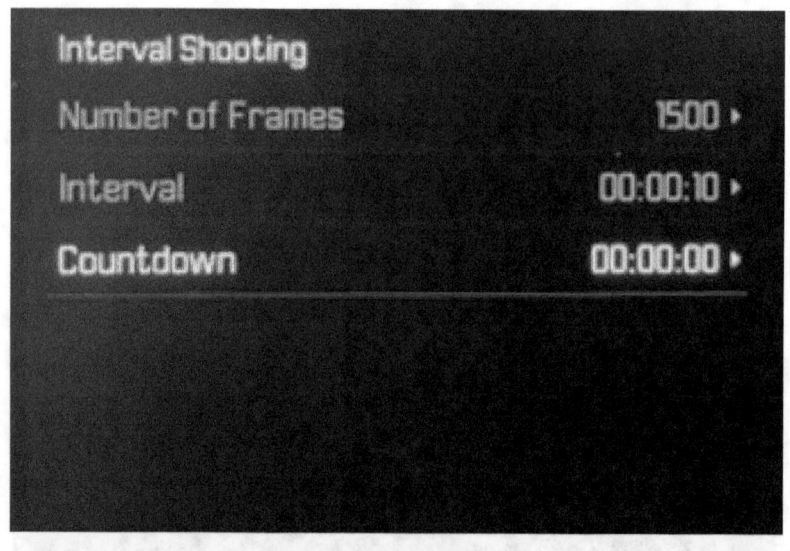

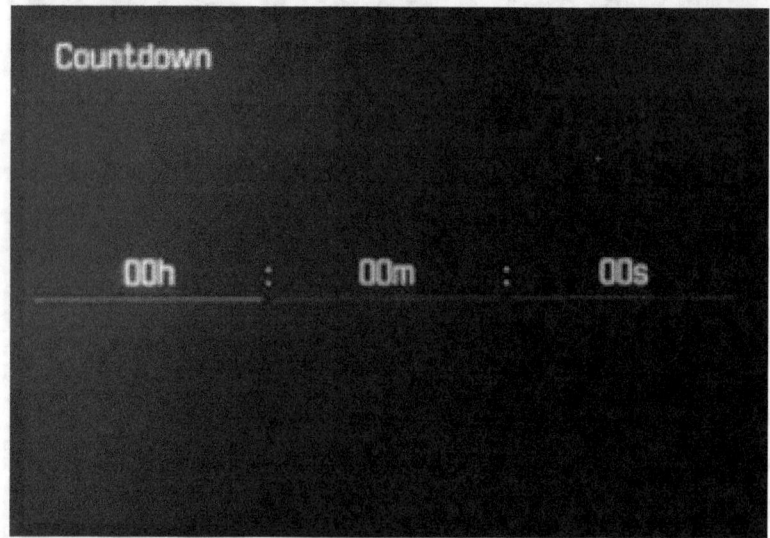

Getting started

➢ Take a picture by pressing the button.

- The screen turns off after each shot but can be turned back on by tapping the button.

- The time left until the next photo and its number appear at the top right.

Canceling a running series of shots

1. Tap the PLAY button.

2. A little menu will show up.

3. Choose "End."

Note:

- If you use autofocus while taking pictures at intervals, some shots may not focus on the same thing.

- If your camera's "Auto power off" setting is on and there's no other activity between shots, the camera might turn off and back on.

- Shooting pictures at intervals for a long time in very cold, hot, or humid conditions might cause the camera to malfunction.

- Interval shooting will stop or be canceled if the battery runs out, or if you turn it off, check the battery to ensure it has enough charge.

- If you stop or pause the repeated photo-taking (interval shooting) on your camera, you can resume it by turning it off, changing the battery or memory card if needed, and turning it back on. A message will pop up if you do this while the interval shooting is still active.

- The interval shooting function stays active even after you've taken the photos and if you turn the camera off and on again until you switch to another shooting mode.

- Just because the camera can do interval shooting doesn't mean it's meant for continuous monitoring.

- When you review the photos, the last one taken or saved will show up first, no matter how many photos were in the series.

- Interval shots are labeled with a timer icon in preview mode.

- If the camera can't take a good picture due to unsuccessful focusing, it won't take that picture, and the series will continue with the next interval. A message saying "Some Frames are dropped" will appear.

Exposure bracketing

Some beautiful things have both bright and dark parts. When taking pictures, adjusting the camera to these different areas can change the photo a lot. You can get multiple pictures with different exposures and shutter speeds using the automatic bracketing feature in aperture-priority mode.

Afterward, you can choose your favorite or use photo editing software to create an image with a wide contrast range (HDR).

You can pick 3 or 5 frames and set the exposure difference to 3 EVs using EV Steps.

➤ Go to the main menu and choose Drive Mode.

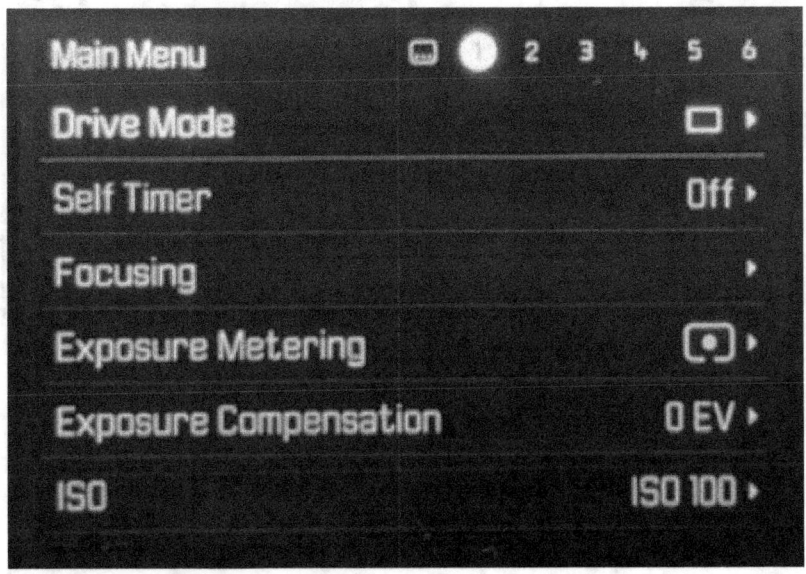

➤ Find and select Exposure Bracketing.

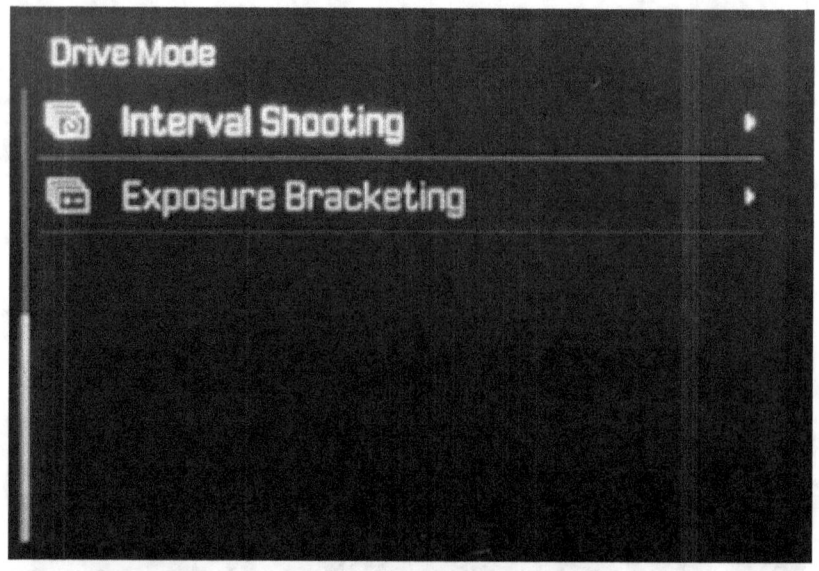

➤ Pick how many pictures you want in Number of Frames.

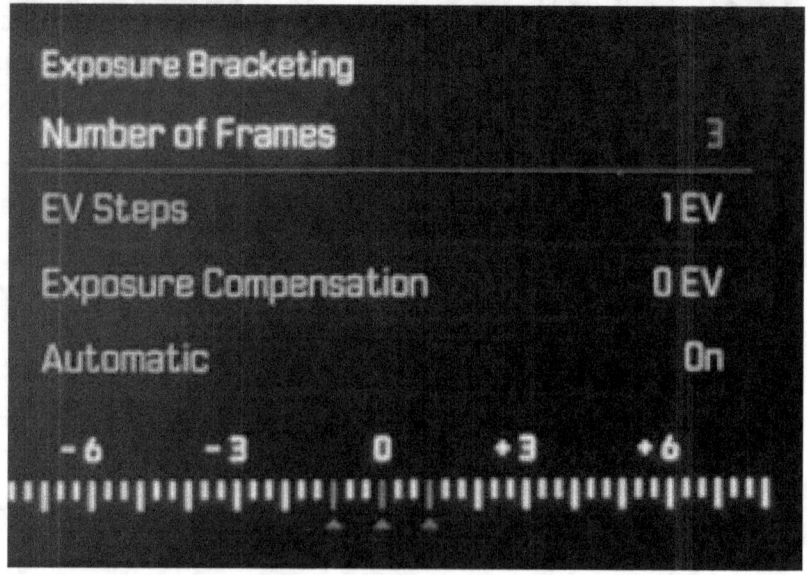

➤ Adjust the exposure difference in EV steps.

➤ Set your desired Exposure Compensation value.

  ○ The marked exposure values and scale change based on your choices.

  ○ The chosen exposure compensation applies to all shots in the series.

➤ Choose an option under Automatic

  ○ With On, all shots run together with one press; with Off, take each picture separately.

➤ Press the shutter button to take one or several shots.

Look for a symbol on the screen to know if bracketing is on. When you take photos, you'll see the effect of bracketing – it can make the picture brighter or darker.

The exposure settings change based on the mode:

- Shutter speed (A/M)

- Aperture (S)

- Shutter speed and aperture value (P)

The shots happen in this order: too dark/correctly exposed/too bright. The range for automatic bracketing might be limited, depending on your shutter speed and aperture choices.

When you use automatic ISO sensitivity control, the camera will keep the same ISO setting for all photos in a series. It might lead to slower shutter speeds, potentially exceeding the limit set. The number of frames in automatic bracketing is fixed, even if some shots have the same exposure. This function continues until you choose a different mode from the Drive menu. Otherwise, it takes a new bracket set each time you press the shutter button.

Self-timer

The Self-timer function in the Leica Q3 is a feature that enables users to capture photos with a delay after pressing the shutter release button. This delay allows the photographer to join the frame or set up the camera for a shot without the need for assistance. The Self-timer is particularly handy for taking self-portraits, group photos, or capturing scenes where the photographer wants to be in the picture.

To take a delayed photo using the self-timer:

1. Go to the main menu and choose "Self-timer."

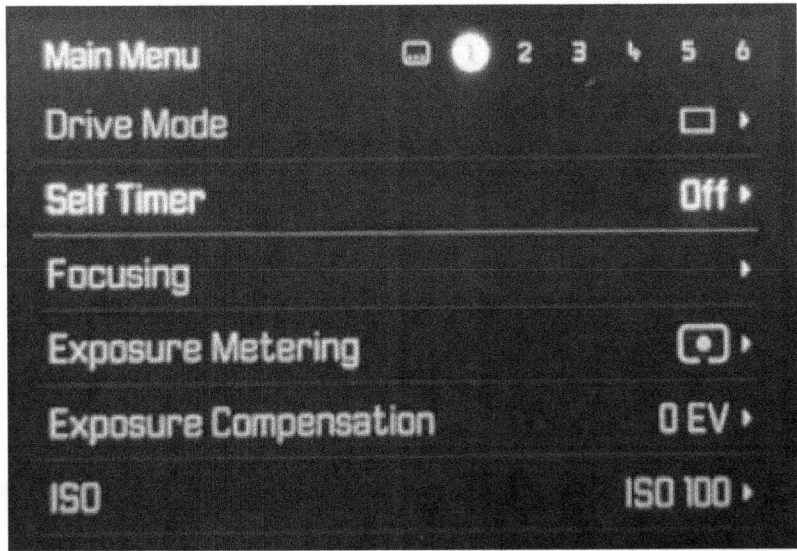

2. Pick either a 2-second or 12-second delay.

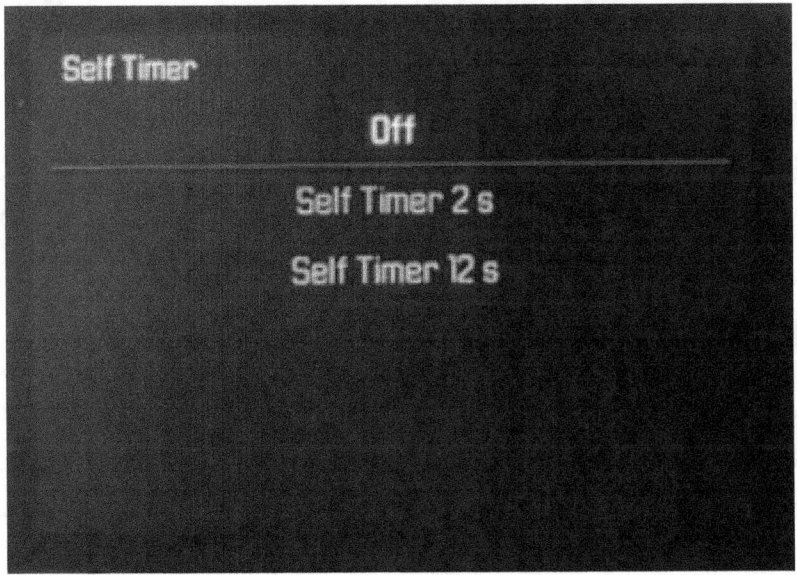

When you press the shutter button:

- The camera displays the time left on the screen.

- A light on the front of the camera counts down, flashing slowly for the first 10 seconds and then quickly for the last 2 seconds.

- You can cancel the delay by tapping the shutter button, and your chosen settings will stay the same.

- First, the camera measures the light exposure, and in autofocus mode, it focuses before starting any delay.

- The self-timer works only for taking one photo at a time and bracketing.

- The self-timer stays on until you pick a different function from the self-timer menu.

Setting Resolution and File Type

File format

Pick between JPG or DNG (digital negative) formats for your photos. JPG is processed in the camera with automatic adjustments like contrast and saturation, providing a quick, optimized preview. DNG, on the other hand, is recommended for post-processing as it retains raw data, allowing more flexibility in adjustments later.

DNG files store all the original camera data when you take a photo. You'll need special software like Adobe Photoshop Lightroom or Capture One Pro to view or edit these files.

Adjusting various settings is possible during post-processing to meet your preferences.

For the factory setting, choose between DNG, DNG + JPG, or JPG formats by navigating to "Picture File Format" in the main menu.

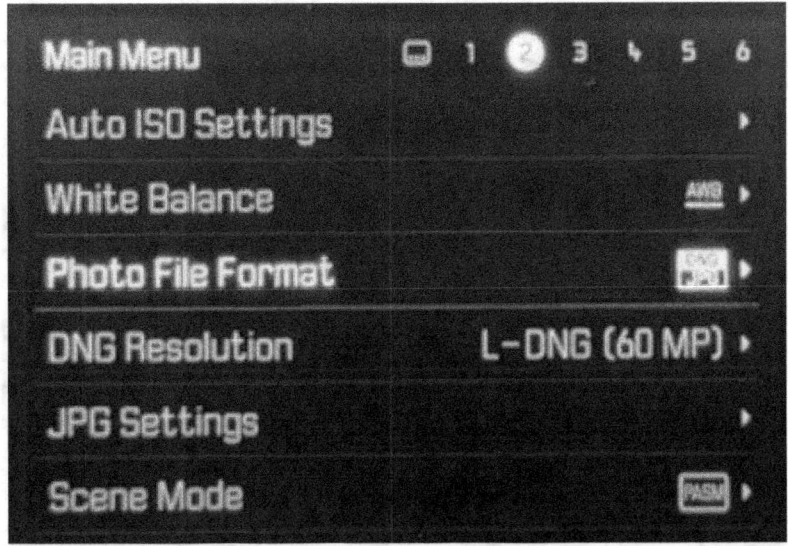

1. Raw image data is stored in a standardized format called DNG.

2. Depending on the subject, the number of shots left on the LCD may change after each photo. Detailed images use more data, while simple surfaces use less.

Resolution

DNG Resolution

The DNG Resolution feature on your camera provides a valuable level of control over the quality and file size of the raw photos you capture. When shooting in raw format, you have the option to select from three different picture qualities: large, medium, and small. Remarkably, even if you opt for a smaller size, the inherent advantages of raw photography, such as rich colors and an expansive tonal range, remain intact.

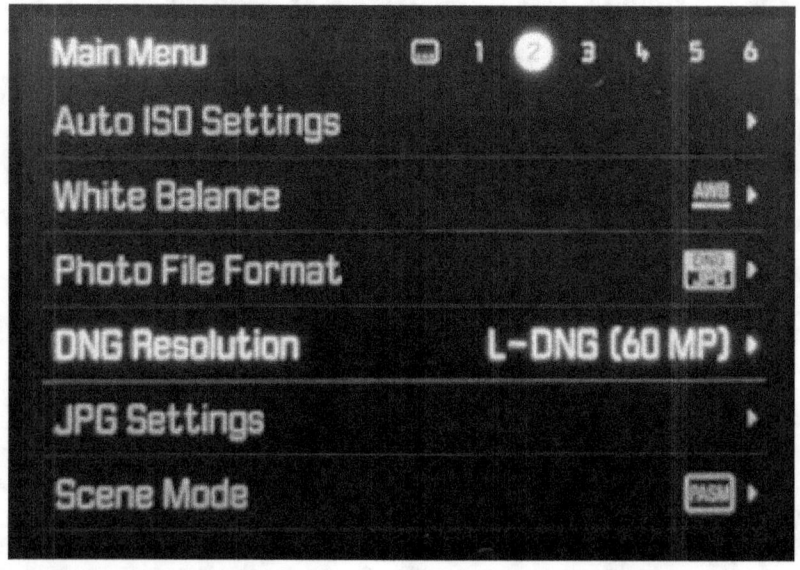

To tailor your DNG Resolution settings, navigate to the main menu of your camera. Within the menu options, locate and select "DNG Resolution." Here, you can choose the specific size you desire for your raw images. The available options include large, with an impressive 60 megapixels (MP), medium, boasting 36 MP, and small, delivering 18 MP. It's worth noting that the default setting is typically large (L-DNG).

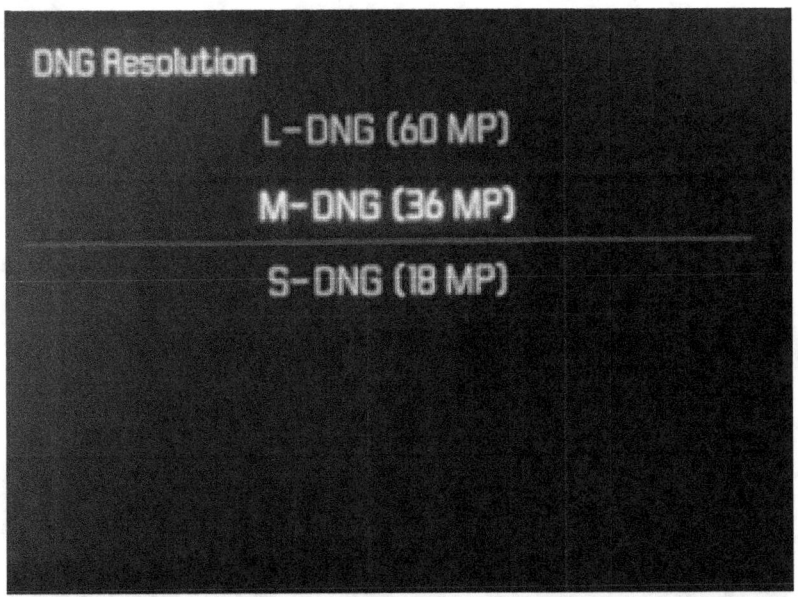

Choosing a specific DNG Resolution allows you to strike a balance between image quality and file size, providing flexibility based on your intended use for the photographs. The large resolution is ideal for scenarios where maximum detail is crucial, while the medium and small options are beneficial when storage space is a consideration or when you don't require the highest resolution.

JPG Resolution

The JPG Resolution feature on your camera provides a range of options to customize the quality and file size of the JPEG images you capture, allowing you to align them with your specific needs and the available capacity of your memory card. This flexibility is particularly valuable for photographers who prioritize storage efficiency or have varying requirements for different shooting scenarios.

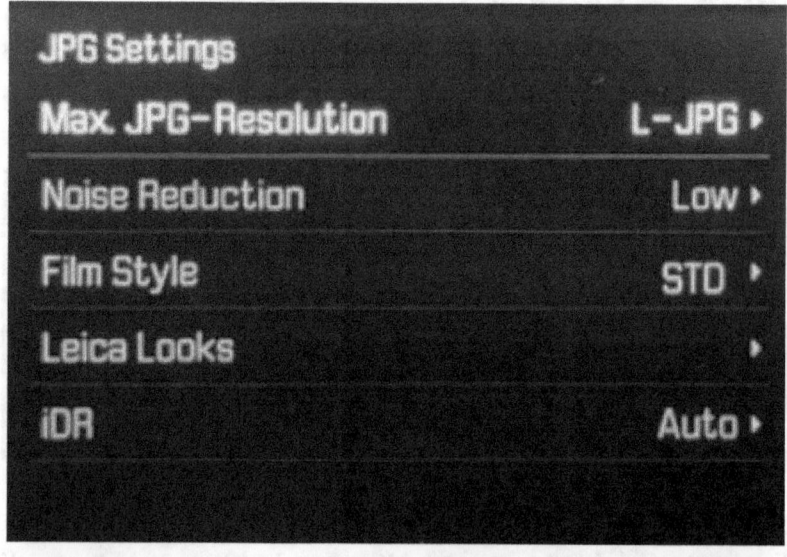

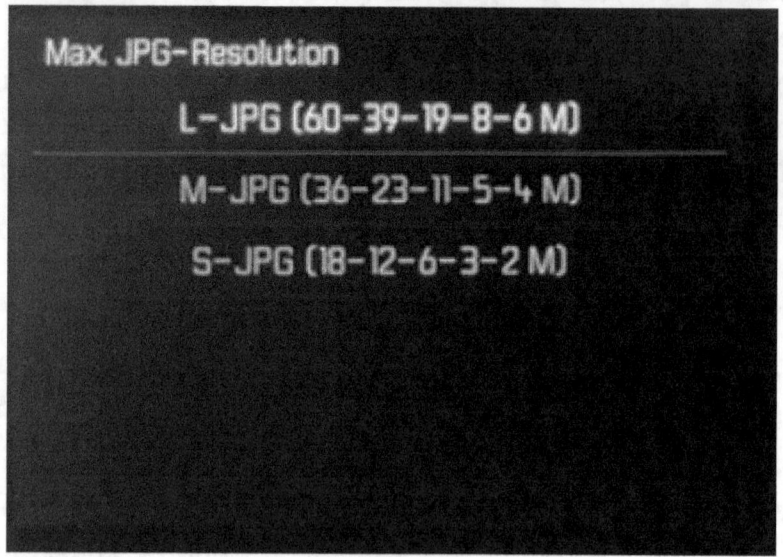

You can choose from three distinct picture quality options: Large (L-JPG), Medium (M-JPG), and Small (S-JPG). Each option caters to different preferences and requirements, providing a balance between image quality and file size. The default setting is typically Large (L-JPG), offering high-resolution images that retain detail and clarity.

To make adjustments to the JPG Resolution settings, navigate to the main menu of your camera. Within the menu options, locate and select "JPG Settings." Subsequently, go to "JPG Resolution" and pick your preferred resolution size. This step-by-step process empowers you to easily tailor the output of your JPEG images based on your specific shooting needs.

Moreover, it's essential to note that when utilizing Digital Zoom, the camera will save images with specific resolutions. This consideration ensures that even when employing zoom functionality, the resulting images maintain a consistent level of quality and resolution as per your chosen settings.

Main Menu   1 2 3 4 5 6

Auto Review   Off ›

Long exposure noise reduction   On

Customize Control   ›

Digital Zoom   28 ›

User Profile   ›

Capture Assistants   ›

Digital Zoom	JPG Resolution		
	L-JPG	M-JPG	S-JPG
Off (28mm)	60MP	36MP	18MP
35mm	39MP	23MP	12MP
50mm	19MP	11MP	6MP
75mm	8MP	5MP	3MP

90mm	6MP	4MP	2MP

Aspect Ratio

The Aspect Ratio feature on your camera introduces a creative dimension to your photography by allowing you to select different picture shapes based on your artistic preferences and the specific requirements of your compositions. This feature goes beyond the default rectangular shape (3:2) and offers alternative options such as square (1:1) or wide (16:9), enabling you to experiment with various visual formats.

When opting for a particular Aspect Ratio, the resulting JPG images will conform to the chosen shape. For instance, selecting the square aspect ratio will yield images in a perfect square format (1:1), while the wide aspect ratio will produce images with a cinematic widescreen feel (16:9). This customization empowers photographers to craft images that align with their creative vision and suit the intended presentation format, whether for social media, prints, or other display mediums.

It's important to note that when shooting in DNG format, the original aspect ratio (3:2) is preserved in the raw images. The chosen aspect ratio in this case serves as a composition guide, allowing you to visualize the desired framing while capturing the full sensor data. Consequently, when reviewing DNG photos, you may notice lines indicating the cropped section based on the chosen aspect ratio during shooting. This visual guide assists in post-processing, providing a reference for how the final composition will look in a different aspect ratio.

To set:

1. Go to "Photo Aspect Ratio" in the main menu.

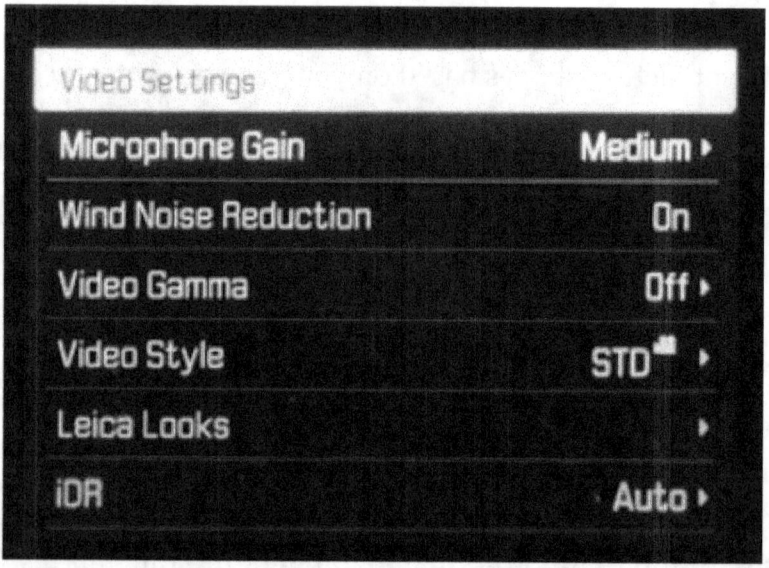

2. Pick your preferred shape: 3:2, 4:3, 1:1, or 16:9.

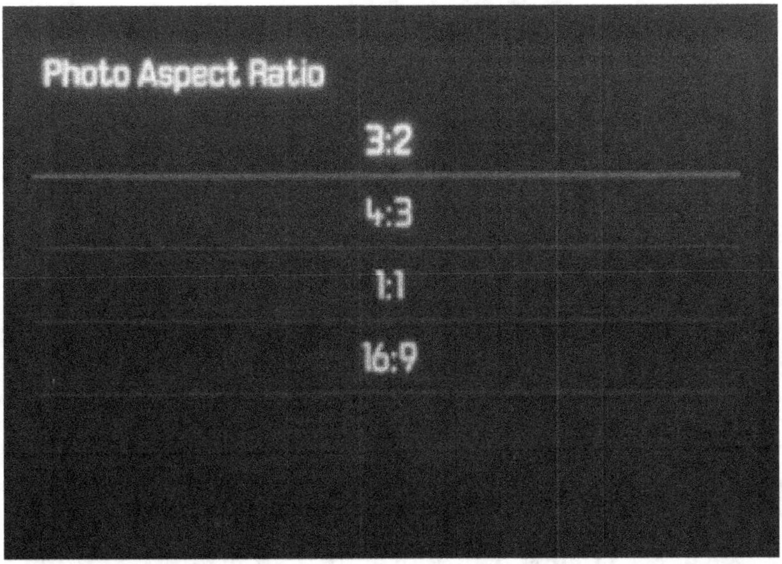
Photo Aspect Ratio
3:2
4:3
1:1
16:9

CHAPTER 4: TAKING GREAT PICTURES AUTOMATICALLY

Flash Photography

The camera uses pre-flashes to determine how much flash a photo needs. Then, it takes the photo with the main flash, considering factors like filters, aperture, distance, and reflective surfaces.

Compatible Flash Units

The Leica Q3 is specifically designed to seamlessly integrate with compatible flash units, offering advanced features such as TTL (Through-The-Lens) flash exposure. Among the recommended flash units for optimal performance are the Leica SF40 and Profoto models. These units have been tested and calibrated to work harmoniously with the camera's sophisticated technology, ensuring accurate and consistent flash exposures.

It's important to note that while the Leica Q3 is equipped with a positive center contact to support a range of flash units, the camera may not be able to exert control over non-compatible units. In other words, using flash units other than the recommended Leica SF40 or Profoto models may result in limited functionality, and the camera might not be able to regulate aspects such as flash intensity or synchronization.

The absence of seamless integration with non-compatible flash units does not necessarily mean they cannot be physically attached to the Leica Q3; however, the camera's ability to optimize flash settings and deliver precise exposures may be compromised. This limitation underscores the importance of using the recommended flash units to fully leverage the camera's capabilities.

Important Points:

1. If you're using a flash that isn't made for your camera, manually set the camera's white balance.

2. Using an incompatible flash with your Leica Q3 could permanently damage the camera or flash.

3. Ensure your flash is ready to avoid exposure issues or error messages.

4. Studio or RF-controlled flashes may need a slower shutter speed to sync correctly. It also helps prevent delays.

5. Serial exposures and automatic bracketing with flash are not supported.

6. Use a tripod to prevent blur at slow shutter speeds, or choose a higher sensitivity setting.

Attaching the Flash Unit

1. Turn off the camera and flash.

2. Remove and safely store the accessory shoe cover.

3. Slide the flash unit's foot into the accessory shoe and secure it with the clamping nut (if available) to prevent accidental movement.

Remember, movement in the accessory shoe can cause malfunctions by interrupting necessary contacts.

Detaching the Flash Unit

- Turn off the camera and flash.

- Unlock as required.

- Remove the flash.

- Put on the accessory shoe cover.

Always keep the accessory shoe cover on when you're not using accessories like a flash unit.

Flash Exposure Metering (TTL Metering)

The camera works with certain flash units and has an automatic flash mode in the Aperture Priority and Manual modes. In Aperture Priority and Manual modes, you can also use excellent flash techniques like synchronization and slower shutter speeds than the maximum sync time.

The camera tells the flash how sensitive it is to light. The flash then adjusts its range based on this info, but only if the camera has certain displays and if you manually set the lens aperture on the flash. You can't change the ISO setting with the flash on some systems because the camera sends this info to the flash.

Settings on the Flash Unit

Operating mode	
TTL	Automatic control by the camera
A	SF40, SF60: Automatic camera control, no flash exposure compensation SF58, SF64: Control via the flash unit using a built-in exposure sensor
M	The flash exposure must be set to an output level to match the aperture and shutter speed settings determined by the camera.*

Instructions:

1. Ensure the flash is in TTL mode for automatic control by the camera.

2. If set to A, the camera may not correctly expose objects with extreme brightness.

3. Refer to the manual for third-party flash units to understand their different modes.

Flash Modes

Flash modes provide photographers with essential control over how the camera's flash system operates, allowing them to adapt to various lighting conditions and creative preferences. Choose one of these three operating modes: Automatic, Manual, or Long-term exposure.

Automatic Flash Activation

The Automatic Flash Activation feature on your camera serves as the default setting for the flash functionality, ensuring that the flash system automatically engages in situations where the available ambient light is insufficient. This proactive approach is designed to address the challenges of low-light conditions, where slow shutter speeds could potentially lead to blurry photos.

When the camera detects insufficient ambient light, the automatic flash activation comes into play, providing an additional burst of artificial light to illuminate the scene. This serves a dual purpose: firstly, it helps maintain a sufficiently fast shutter speed to freeze motion and prevent motion blur, and secondly, it enhances the overall visibility and clarity of the subject in dimly lit environments.

Manual Flash Activation

This mode is great for photos with strong backlighting, where the main subject is in the shadow or doesn't fill the entire frame. It's also helpful in situations with harsh contrasts, like direct sunlight. The flash fires with every photo, adjusting its intensity based on the existing light. In low light, it's like automatic mode, and as the light increases, the flash output decreases. It acts as a fill-in light, brightening dark areas in the foreground or backlight, creating a more balanced overall look.

Automatic Flash Activation at Slower Shutter Speeds (Long-term Synchronization)

Choose "Flash Settings" in the main menu, then pick "Flash Mode" and choose your desired setting. This mode ensures dark backgrounds are bright enough without making the foreground too bright. It allows slower shutter speeds to prevent underexposed backgrounds but be aware that it might lead to some blurring in other flash modes. The currently active mode is shown on the screen.

Flash Range

Your aperture and sensitivity settings determine the camera's flash range. Make sure your subject is within this range for good lighting. Avoid setting a permanent short flash sync time, as it might cause some parts of your subject to be underexposed. This camera lets you adjust the flash mode shutter speed and aperture, giving you control based on the object or your creative preferences.

Reset the camera to its default settings by choosing "Auto" as the factory setting.

Then, go to the main menu and select "Auto ISO Settings."

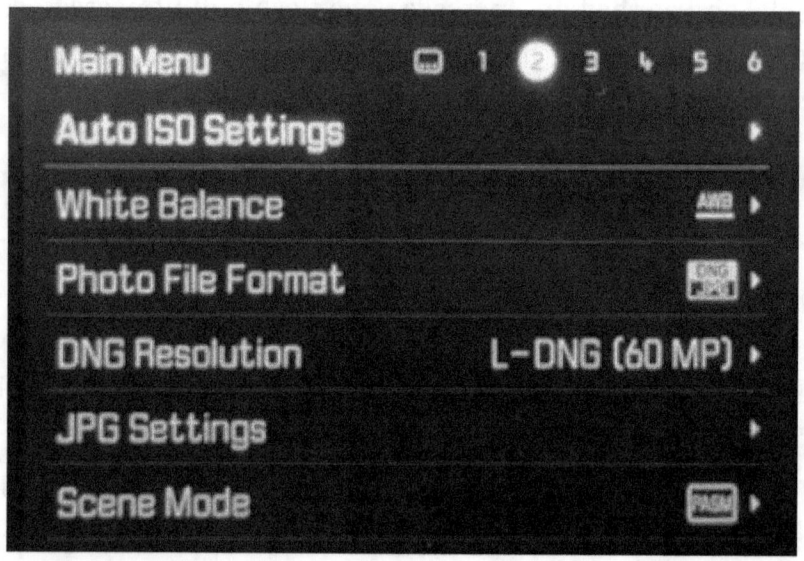

After that, choose "Shutter Speed Limit (Flash)" and pick your preferred speed from options like "Auto," "1/2000," "1/1000," and so on.

The option "Shutter Speed Limit (Flash)" in the "Flash Settings" menu works the same as the one with the same name in the "Auto ISO Settings" menu. Changing it in one menu will also change it in the other.

Flash Exposure Compensation

This feature helps you adjust the brightness of the flash in photos, making a person's face brighter in the foreground while keeping the overall lighting mood the same, especially when taking pictures outdoors in the evening. The default setting is 0, and you can change it by going to the main menu, selecting "Flash Settings," then choosing "Flash Exposure Compensation" to set the desired brightness level.

Once you set compensation values, they stay in effect until you manually reset them to 0, even if you turn the camera off and on again.

- If you're using a flash unit like the Leica SF26, where you can't manually adjust the compensation, you can only use the camera's Flash Exp. Compensation option.

- But if you're using flash units like Leica SF58 or SF60 with their compensation function, the camera's Flash Exp. Compensation won't work, and any adjustment on the camera won't affect the flash.

- Making your flash brighter with Plus compensation means more intensity, impacting the flash range. Plus, correction shortens it, while Minus correction extends it.

- Camera exposure compensation only affects ambient light. If you want to adjust flash exposure in tandem with the camera setting, you must separately set it on the flash unit.

Exploring Scene Modes

Choose from 10 automatic settings in the Scene Modes menu for easy photography. Each setting automatically adjusts the shutter speed and aperture, like the normal automatic program (P). These modes provide other options for specific scenes, such as ISO or focusing.

To use:

1. Go to the main menu and select "Scene Mode."

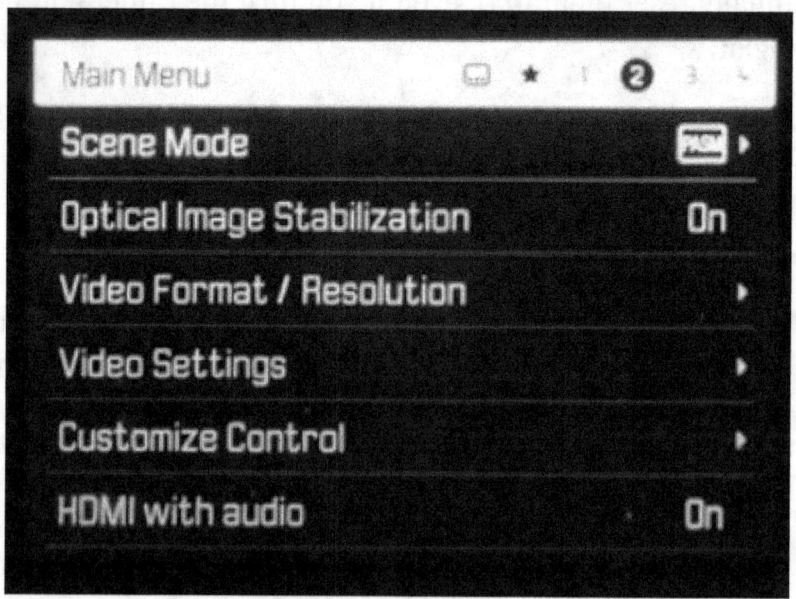

2. Choose the setting you want:

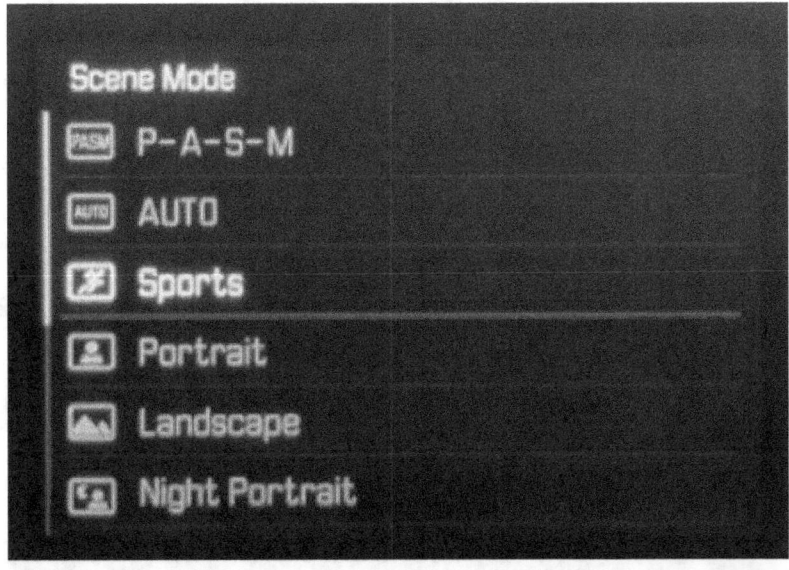

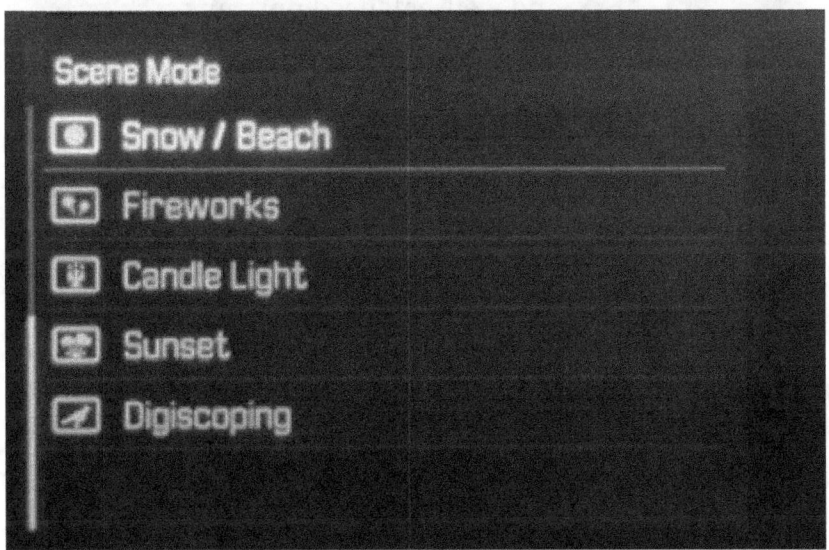

- AUTO: Automatic snapshot for general use

- 9 scene modes for common scenes like Sports, Portrait, Landscape, etc:

- **Sport Mode**

    Purpose: Designed for capturing fast-paced action and sports scenes.

    Key Features: Faster shutter speeds to freeze motion, continuous autofocus to track moving subjects, and optimized exposure settings for dynamic and high-speed situations.

- **Portrait Mode**

    Purpose: Ideal for capturing compelling and well-balanced portraits.

    Key Features: Typically employs a wider aperture to achieve a shallow depth of field, emphasizing the subject while creating a pleasing background blur (bokeh). Skin tones are often enhanced for natural and flattering portraits.

- **Landscape Mode:**

    Purpose: Tailored for shooting expansive landscapes and scenic vistas.

    Key Features: Optimized settings for maximizing depth of field, ensuring sharpness from the foreground to the background. Colors and contrast may be enhanced to capture the beauty of landscapes.

- **Night Portrait Mode**

    Purpose: Suited for capturing portraits in low-light or nighttime conditions.

    Key Features: Balances ambient light with flash, ensuring well-exposed portraits while preserving the atmosphere of the nighttime scene. May use slower sync speeds to capture more ambient light.

- **Snow/Beach Mode**

    Purpose: Designed for shooting in environments with intense brightness, such as snowy landscapes or beach scenes.

    Key Features: Adjusts exposure and white balance settings to prevent overexposure in bright conditions, ensuring accurate and natural-looking images in environments with reflective surfaces.

- **Fireworks Mode**

    Purpose: Tailored for photographing fireworks displays.

Key Features: Uses slower shutter speeds to capture the trails of light created by fireworks. Optimized exposure settings for vibrant and well-defined fireworks against the night sky.

■ Candle Light Mode

Purpose: Ideal for capturing scenes illuminated primarily by candlelight.

Key Features: Adjusts white balance and exposure settings to render warm and atmospheric images by the soft glow of candlelight. Typically uses wider apertures for better light sensitivity.

■ Sunset Mode

Purpose: Optimized for capturing the rich colors and dramatic lighting of sunsets.

Key Features: Adjusts color balance and exposure settings to enhance the warm tones of a sunset, delivering vivid and visually striking images.

■ Digiscoping Mode

Purpose: Tailored for use with spotting scopes or telescopes, often used in birdwatching or nature observation.

Key Features: Optimizes settings for digiscoping, ensuring clear and well-exposed images when capturing distant subjects through an attached optical device.

Detailed information about these functions is provided in the following sections.

1. Once you pick a program, it stays on until you choose a different one, even if you turn off the camera.

2. If you change from Photo to Video mode, the Scene Mode returns to P-A-S-M.

3. You can't use program shift and some menu options.

4. The shutter speed dial and aperture ring don't work.

5. Use a tripod for Digiscoping.

6. Exposure preview works in all programs.

CHAPTER 5: TAKING CHARGE OF EXPOSURE

Introducing the Exposure

Shutter speed

Shutter speed is the amount of time the camera's shutter remains open to allow light to reach the camera's image sensor. It is a crucial component of exposure control and plays a significant role in determining the outcome of your photographs.

You can adjust the shutter speed in two ways:

1. Use the shutter speed dial for big changes.

2. Use the thumbwheel for small adjustments in thirds.

Shutter-speed dial	Thumbwheel
All settings from 2 to 1000	Fine tuning the shutter speed in ⅓EV increments, max. ±⅔EV
Set to 1+	Longer shutter speeds than 1s (0.6s to 120s in ⅓EV increments)

Set to 2000	Shorter shutter speeds than 1⁄1000s (1⁄1250s to 1⁄16000s in 1⁄3EV increments)

Examples of Shutter Speed Fine Tuning Settings

Adjusting the shutter speed to 1/125s and moving the thumbwheel one click left makes it 1/100s. Similarly, setting the shutter speed to 1/500s and moving the thumbwheel two clicks right results in 1/800s.

You can also adjust settings on the status screen instead of using the thumbwheel, depending on how it's set up. In some cases, it might be your only choice.

Long-term Exposure

Long-term exposure, also known as long exposure, in the context of the Leica Q3, refers to capturing a photograph with an extended duration of shutter speed. This technique involves keeping the camera's shutter open for a prolonged period, allowing more light to reach the image sensor. Long-term exposure is often used to achieve creative effects and capture scenes that involve low light or motion.

Fixed Shutter Speeds

Your Leica Q3 camera lets you take pictures with shutter speeds up to 2 minutes in certain modes. After pressing the shutter button, the time left for the exposure is shown on the display in seconds for speeds longer than 1 second.

- Turn the shutter-speed dial to the setting labeled 1+

- Fine-tune and pick your preferred shutter speed

- Press the shutter button to take the photo

T Function

Keep the shutter open in this mode by pressing the shutter button once. It stays open for around 2 minutes, depending on ISO.

- Turn the shutter-speed dial to 1+

- Choose a specific aperture on the aperture ring

- Set the shutter speed to T (requires adjusting it precisely)

- Press the shutter release to start capturing.

Shutter speed depends on the Shutter Type setting. T function works only with Mechanical or Hybrid settings. After taking a long exposure, the remaining time is shown on the display in seconds.

Noise Reduction

You might notice more image noise when you use high camera sensitivities, especially in dark areas. If you take pictures with a slow shutter speed and high ISO, the camera automatically captures a second "dark frame" with the shutter closed. It helps reduce annoying noise in the photo by digitally subtracting the noise from the dark frame. You'll see a message saying "Noise reduction in progress..." along with a time estimate during this process.

Remember to adjust for the doubled exposure time for long exposure shots and keep the camera on. It's advisable to turn off Noise Reduction to take multiple consecutive shots and apply noise reduction during editing. Use raw data format for the images.

If certain conditions are met, noise reduction is always active with the T function and exposures ≥+8s. Otherwise, noise reduction depends on factors like ISO, exposure time, and sensor temperature. Refer to the table for typical shutter speeds and when noise reduction is applied at 25°C.

ISO	Shutter speed longer than
100	7 s
200	6.4 s
400	5.9 s

800	5.4 s
1600	4.9 s
3200	4.5 s
6400	4.2 s
≥12500	3.8 s

ISO sensitivity

The ISO setting on your camera goes from 50 to 100000, letting you adjust to different situations. If you use automatic ISO, you have more flexibility with shutter speed and aperture, and you can also set priorities for better picture composition. The default is usually Auto ISO.

Fixed ISO Values

Choose ISO settings between 50 and 100,000 in 14 steps. For manual settings, start with whole steps; from ISO 50,000, use 1/3 steps. Go to the main menu, pick ISO, and choose your preferred value.

Using high ISO settings or editing the picture later, you might see image noise and stripes in bigger, evenly lit parts of the object.

Automatic Setting

The camera changes its sensitivity based on the brightness and settings you choose for the shutter speed and aperture. This feature widens the range for automatic exposure control when using aperture-priority mode. You can set the ISO sensitivity automatically in small steps. To do this, go to the main menu, choose ISO, and then select Auto ISO.

Limiting Setting Ranges

You can choose the highest ISO value and set a maximum exposure time. There are automatic and fixed options for shutter speeds (1/2s and 1/2000s). Different settings are there for using Flash.

Limiting ISO Values

You can choose any ISO setting from 200 onwards. The default is 6400. To change it, go to Auto ISO Settings in the main menu, select Maximum ISO, and pick your preferred value.

Limiting Shutter Speed Ranges

Set your camera to its default settings by choosing "Auto" in the factory settings. To adjust the ISO settings, go to the main menu and select "Auto ISO Settings." Then, choose "Shutter Speed Limit" and pick the preferred value from options like Auto, 1/2000, 1/1000, etc.

Limiting ISO Values (Flash)

You can choose any ISO value from 200 and up. The default is 6400. To set the maximum ISO for Flash, go to Auto ISO Settings in the main menu and select Maximum ISO. Choose the value you want.

Limiting Shutter Speed Ranges (Flash)

To reset:

1. Go to the main menu.

2. Choose "Auto ISO Settings."

3. Select "Shutter Speed Limit (Flash)."

4. Pick your preferred value from options like Auto, 1/2000, 1/1000, etc.

Dynamic ISO Setting

You can easily set the ISO manually using the thumbwheel, and it will go through all the options in the ISO menu, including Auto ISO.

Exposure Control

Exposure Preview

The screen brightness shows how your photo will look based on the chosen settings when you press the shutter button halfway. It helps you see the impact of exposure settings before taking the photo, but it will only work if the brightness is high enough.

You can turn off this feature in manual mode (M). The default setting is P-A-S-M.

To enable:

1. Go to the main menu.

2. Choose "Exposure Preview."

3. Select P-A-S (only in certain modes) or P-A-S-M (also for manual mode).

Notes

The screen might show images differently based on the lighting around you. Despite your settings, the screen image may look darker than the actual picture, especially in long-exposure situations. Also, the exposure preview will appear if you use a different control (like a function button) for exposure metering.

Exposure Lock

When taking pictures, we often place essential things away from the center. These elements might be bright or dark. However, some camera settings focus on the center and an average color. Exposure lock helps by measuring the main subject first and saving those settings until you can capture the whole image. It also works for focusing. tNormally, you do both (focusing and exposure) when pressing the shutter button. But you can split these functions between the shutter button and another button, like a function button. These functions involve adjusting and saving settings.

AE-L (Auto Exposure Lock)

Auto Exposure Lock (AE-L) is a valuable feature found on many cameras, including the Leica Q3. This function allows you to lock the exposure settings based on a specific scene or subject, even if you choose to recompose the shot or focus on a different area.

AF-L (Auto Focus Lock)

Auto Focus Lock (AF-L) is a convenient feature on many cameras, including the Leica Q3, designed to enhance your control over focus settings. This function allows you to lock the focus at a specific point, even if you decide to recompose your shot or if your subject moves within the frame.

AE-L/AF-L

The AE-L/AF-L setting, often found on digital cameras like the Leica Q3, stands for Auto Exposure Lock / Auto Focus Lock. This feature is designed to enhance control and flexibility in exposure and focus settings. When activated, the camera memorizes specific exposure and focus parameters, making it particularly useful in various shooting scenarios.

Note: Using an exposure lock with multi-field metering won't work well for capturing specific objects. If you manually adjust the aperture or shutter speed, any exposure lock you had set before will be canceled.

Exposure Compensation

Like an average image, exposure meters are set for a medium gray scale. If your picture is too bright or dark, you can adjust it using exposure compensation. It is handy when taking multiple shots with slightly different exposures; the adjustment stays in place until you change it. You can tweak exposure in small steps, from -3 to +3.

Using thumbwheel control

Choose "Customize Control" from the main menu, then pick "Wheel Assignment," go to "Exp. Comp.," and adjust the value using the thumbwheel.

Using menu control

Choose "Exposure Compensation" from the main menu. A scale will show up on the screen, and you can adjust the value on the scale. The chosen value will be shown above the scale.

Note: Adjusting the setting makes the screen either darker or lighter. Once you choose compensation values, they stay in effect until you manually reset them to zero, even if you turn the camera off and on. You can check the set exposure compensation by looking at the mark on the scale at the bottom.

CHAPTER 6: CAPTURING VIDEO

Video Settings

Video Style

You can tweak how videos look by adjusting a few settings. These adjustments are bundled into preset Video Style profiles.

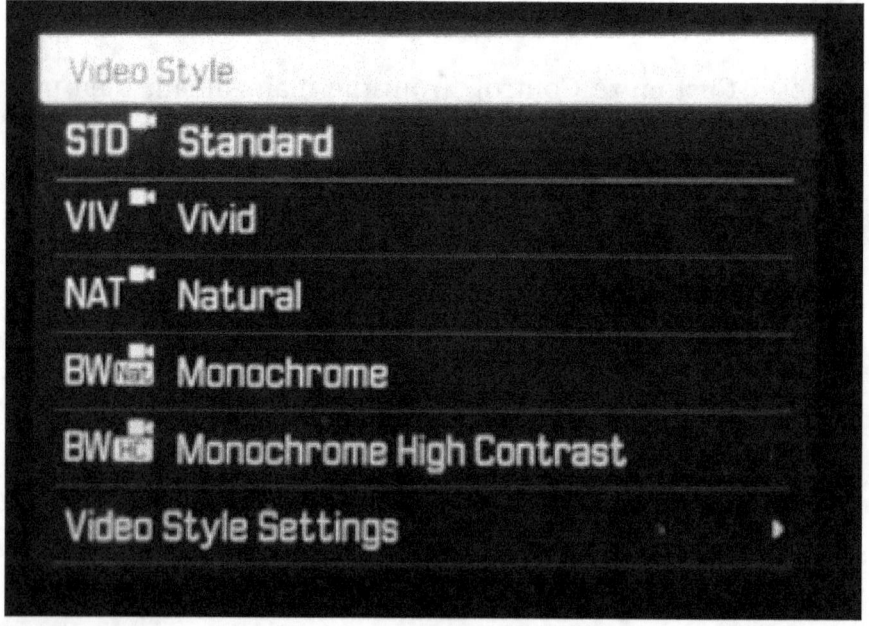

Contrast

The contrast setting decides how much difference there is between the light and dark parts of a picture. Increasing or decreasing this difference makes some parts of the picture look brighter or darker, affecting whether the image looks "flat" or "brilliant."

Sharpness

How sharp a picture looks depends on how clear the edges are, like how smoothly the light and dark parts transition. If you make the transition areas bigger or smaller, it will affect how sharp the picture appears.

Color Saturation

The saturation factor in color images decides if the colors in pictures look soft and pastel or vibrant and colorful. Even though lighting and weather are fixed when taking photos, they can still affect the colors' appearance.

Highlight/Shadow

Depending on how you set things and the range of light and dark in a picture, some details might be hard to see. Highlight and Shadow controls let you adjust bright or not-so-bright parts separately. Turning up the Shadow setting can make it easier to see if something is in shadow. On the other hand, you should make shadows or bright spots stand out more for artistic reasons. Positive values make things brighter, while negative values make them darker.

Color Profile

Choose from three pre-set color options: Standard, Vivid, and Natural. To do this, go to the main menu, select Video Settings, choose Video Style, and pick a profile.

Monochrome Profile

You can choose between two extra styles for black-and-white videos: "Monochrome" and "Monochrome High Contrast." Go to the main menu, pick "Video Settings," then choose "Video Style," and select the style you want.

Customizing Video Profiles

You can change settings for all profiles (except Saturation, which is only for color profiles) by following these steps:

1. Go to Video Settings in the main menu.

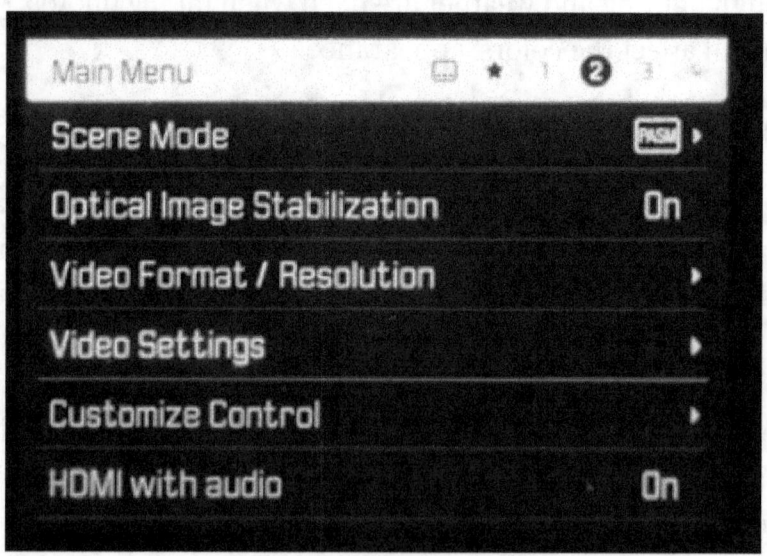

2. Choose Video Style.

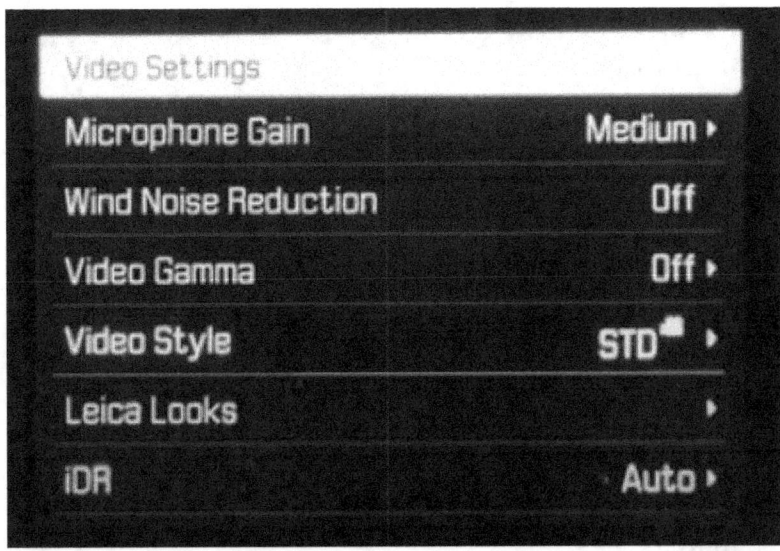

3. Select Video Style Settings.

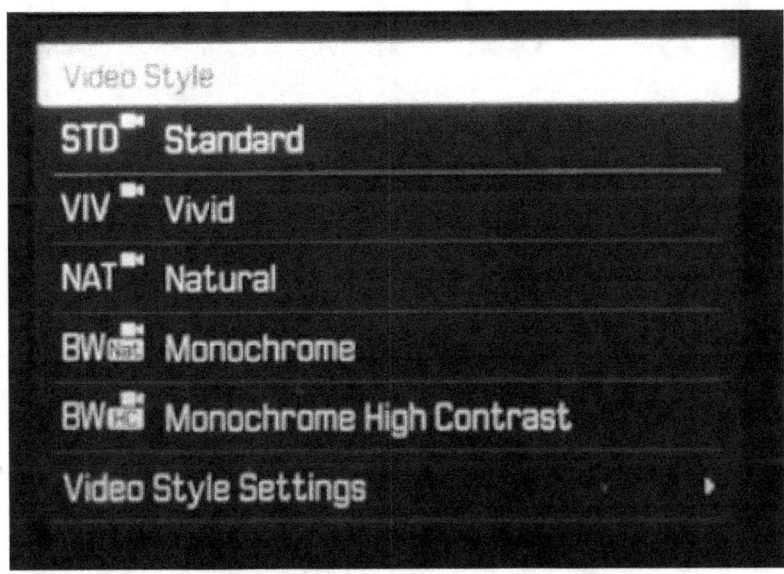

4. Pick a profile.

5. Adjust Contrast, Highlight, Shadow, Sharpness, or Saturation.

6. Choose the desired level (-2, -1, 0, +1, +2).

Audio Settings

Microphone Gain

You can adjust how sensitive the microphone is.

By default, it's set to medium.

To change it:

1. Go to Video Settings in the main menu.

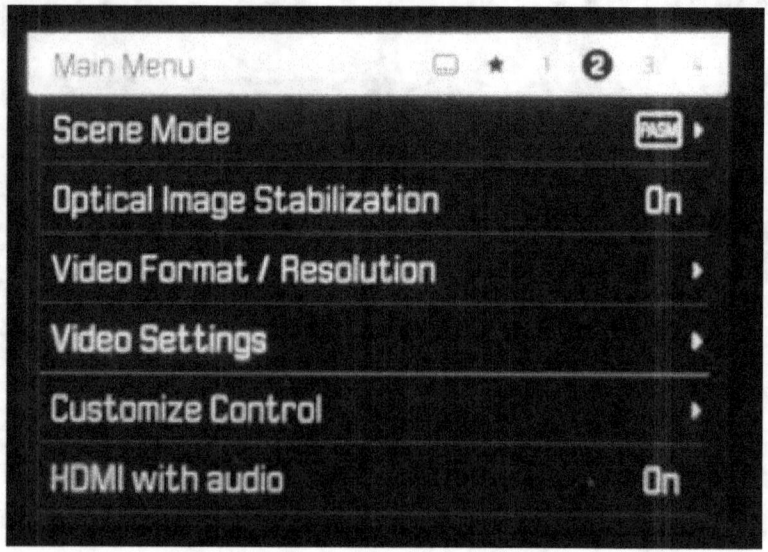

2. Choose Microphone Gain.

3. Pick the level you want (high, medium, low, low, or off).

Autofocus and manual focus tweaks can make noise in the recording. If you turn the setting off, there won't be any audio recorded, and the recording level icon will change to let you know.

Wind Noise Reduction

Wind Noise Reduction is a feature commonly found in audio recording settings on cameras, particularly those with video recording capabilities. Its primary purpose is to minimize or eliminate unwanted wind noise that can be picked up by the camera's built-in microphone during video recording or audio capture.

You can turn Wind Noise Reduction on or off as you like.

By default, it's set to On.

To change it:

1. Go to Video Settings in the main menu.

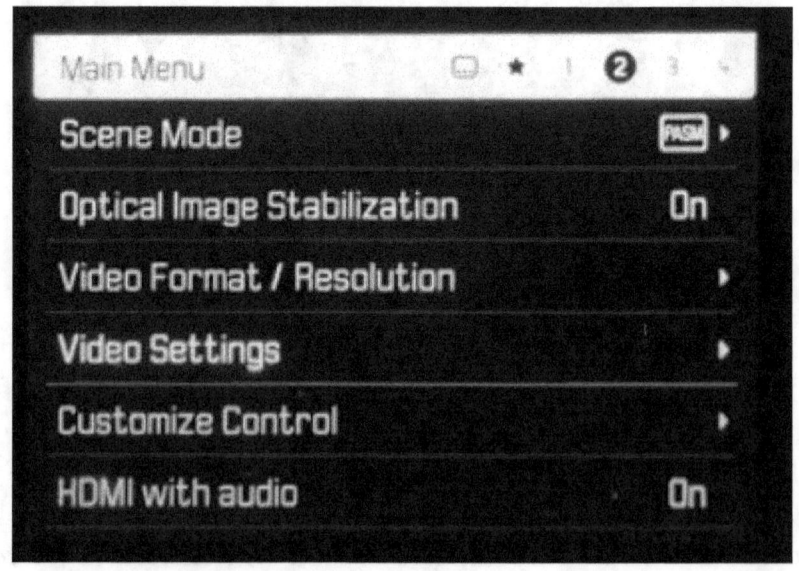

2. Choose Wind Noise Reduction.

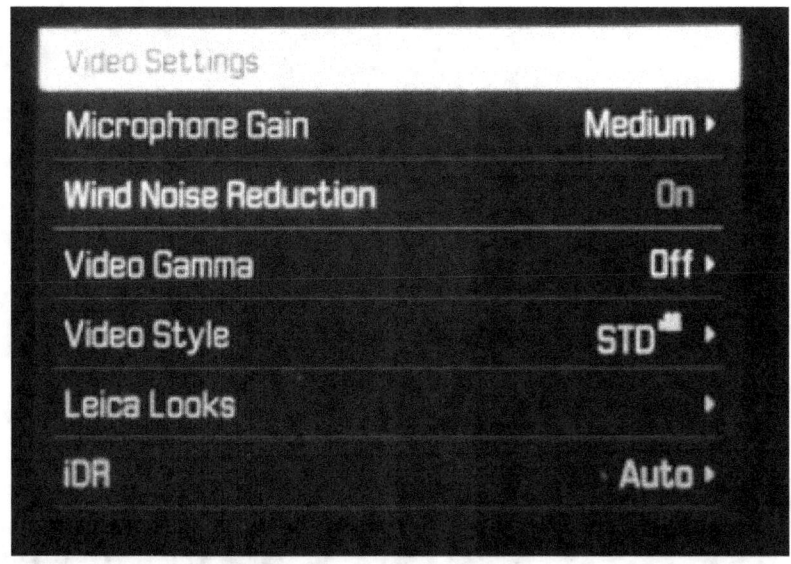

3. Select On or Off.

Video Gamma

You can set the video gamma to HLG or L-Log or turn it off completely.

Off	Optimization for playback compatible with all screen/TV devices in compliance with the BT.709 standard.
HLG	Optimization for HDR-capable UHD-TV devices.
L-Log	Optimization for professional reworking, e.g. color grading.

Initial state: Off

1. Go to Video Settings in the main menu.

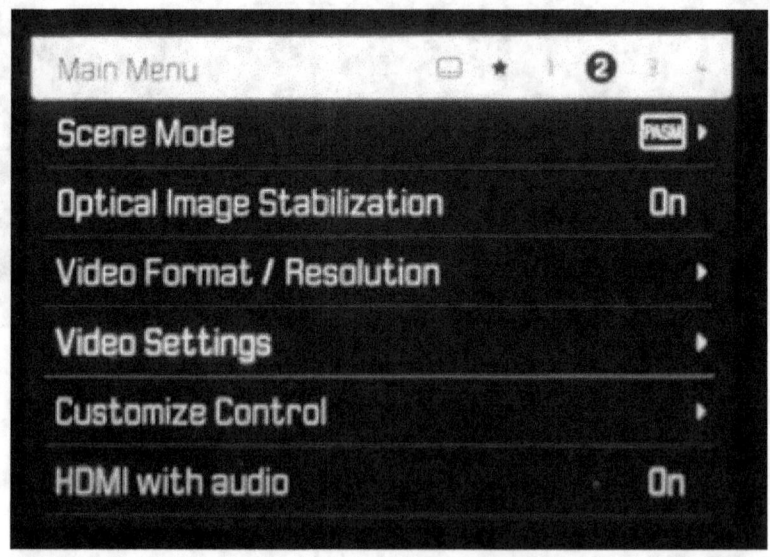

2. Choose Video Gamma.

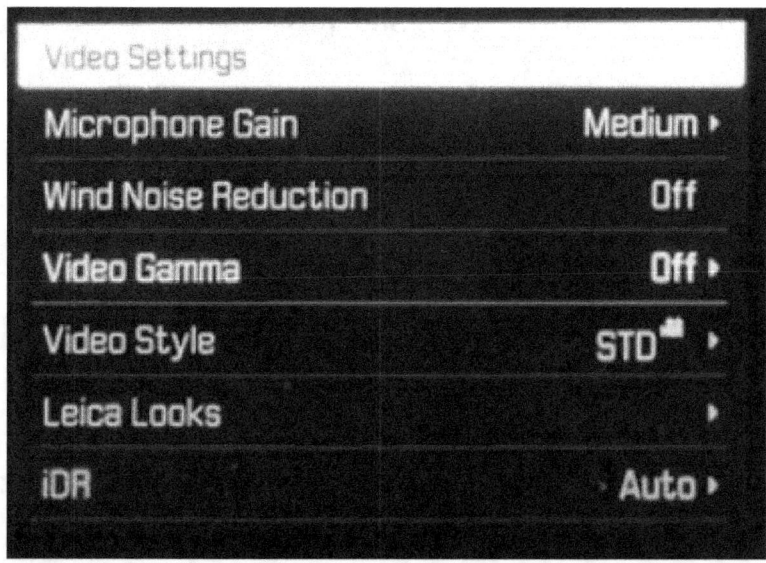

3. Pick your preferred setting: Off, HLG, L-Log.

Video Gamma is not an option when:

- Recording in MP4 format

- Recording in 8-bit

- Recording in slow motion

When using Video Gamma, you can't use:

- iDR

- ISO 50, ISO 100, and ISO 200

- Video Style/Leica Looks

HLG Settings

You can adjust Sharpness and saturation on your device. Go to the main menu and choose Video Settings, Video Gamma, and Settings. From there, select HLG and pick either Sharpness or Saturation. You can set it to -2, -1, 0, +1, or +2 based on your preference. The default is 0.

L-LOG Settings

L-LOG settings, often associated with video recording, typically refer to a Logarithmic or "Log" gamma curve used to capture a wider dynamic range in video footage. Log profiles are known for preserving more information in both shadow and highlight areas, allowing for greater flexibility during color grading in post-production. You can make L-Log sharper, and you can also use different LUT profiles to preview it. Your saved recordings won't change.

Sharpness

Sharpness refers to the degree of contrast between adjacent pixels in an image or video. Adjusting the sharpness setting allows photographers and videographers to control the perceived clarity and crispness of the captured visuals. Reset the factory setting to -2. Go to Video Settings in the main menu, choose Video Gamma, then go to Settings. Select L-Log, and choose Sharpness. Pick your preferred setting from -2 to +2.

Setup/Management of LUT Profiles

You can choose and use your color profiles for the camera to ensure the colors look how you want them. Go to Video Settings, then Video Gamma, and finally select Custom LUT in the Settings. You'll see a list of memory slots for different color profiles, and the filled ones will show the name of the saved profile.

Example

For the upcoming pictures, we'll use the task described below. Two spaces are used for the internal camera display (LCD panel/EVF), and the rest are not used.

Importing a custom LUT profile

1. Get an LUT profile by downloading or exporting it as a CUBE file.

2. Give the file a short and meaningful name (maximum 8 characters) with the file ending ".cub." This name will show up as the profile name in the camera after you import it, and you can't change it later.

3. Save the downloaded file to the memory card, placing it in the main directory (not a sub-directory).

4. Insert the memory card into the camera.

5. Choose an unused memory slot. If none are available, delete an existing profile first.

6. The "Import" dialog will appear, showing the files on the memory card. If the camera doesn't find a compatible file, it will display "Import Failed."

7. Select the profile you want to import.

8. Confirm by selecting "Yes."

Notes

- Only use ".cub" files for importing LUT profiles.

- If you have files ending in ".cube," rename them before saving them to the SD card.

- Keep file names within 8 characters (including spaces).

- Unrecognized or incompatible files won't be acknowledged.

- Up to six profiles on the memory card will be shown, sorted by saving order.

- Some situations may limit the search to only three profile files.

- When using two memory cards, only files on SD1 will be considered if both have compatible files.

Freeing a memory slot

Choose a profile, and then click "Delete." After that, choose "Yes" in the dialog that pops up.

Note: You can't remove the preset profiles Natural and Classic. Also, you can't delete a profile that is currently being used.

Automatic Optimization

Video Stabilization

The stabilization feature prevents shaky videos when you're holding the camera. To turn it on or off, go to the main menu, choose "Optical Image Stabilization," and then select either "On" or "Off."

Dark Area Optimization (IDR)

Dark Area Optimization or IDR (Image Dynamic Range) likely refers to a feature designed to enhance the visibility and detail in dark or shadowed areas of an image. This kind of optimization is aimed at improving the overall dynamic range, ensuring that both highlights and shadows in a photograph are well-represented.

Dynamic Range

The range of brightness in an object, from the brightest to the darkest, is called the contrast range. A camera can capture all these brightness levels if the object's contrast range is within the camera's dynamic range; however, if there are significant differences in brightness, like shooting indoors with bright windows or capturing shadows and direct sunlight outdoors, a camera with a limited dynamic range may not capture the full contrast range. It leads to lost details in the bright and dark areas, known as under and overexposure.

iDR Function

The iDR (Intelligent Dynamic Range) function makes dark areas in photos look better. You can choose how much it does this by setting it to high, standard, or low or turning it off. If you pick Auto, the camera will decide based on the object's contrast.

The effect also depends on exposure settings. It works best with low ISO and fast shutter speeds, less with higher ISO or slower shutter speeds.

By default, it's set to Auto. To change it:

1. Go to Video Settings in the main menu.

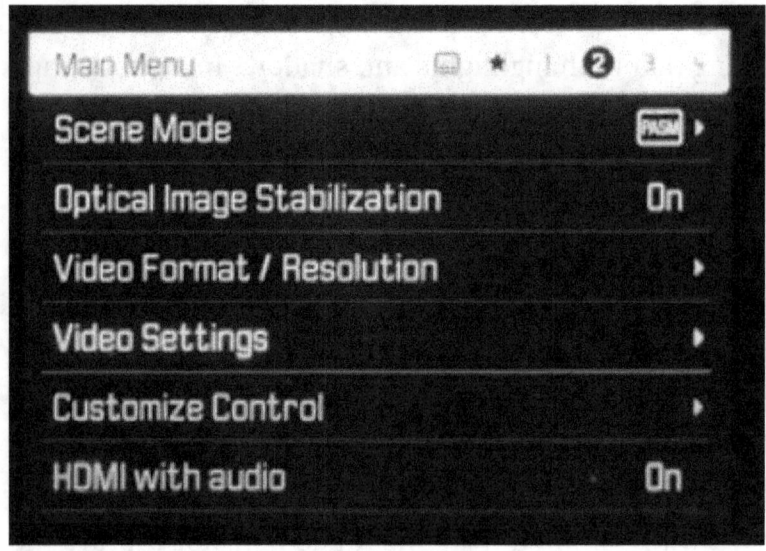

2. Choose iDR.

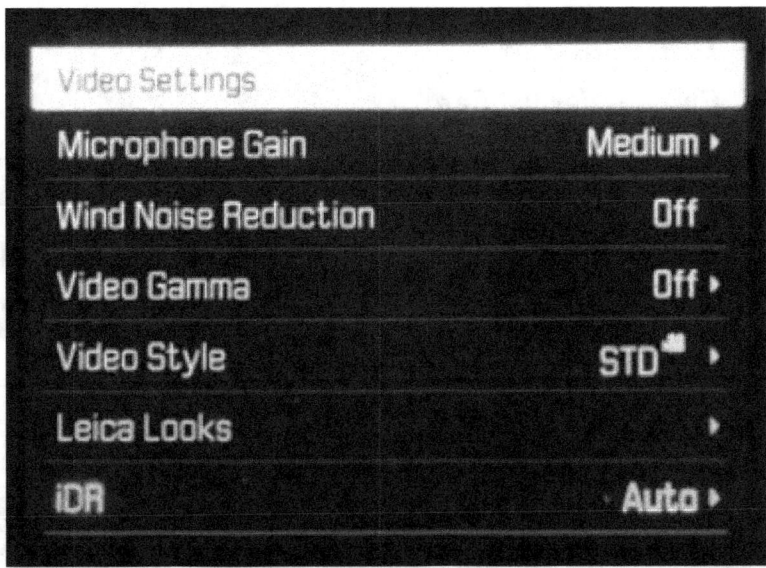

3. Pick your setting (Auto, High, Standard, Low, Off).

Note: Making dark areas look better might make very bright areas less distinct.

Data Management

Formatting a Memory Card

If you've used a memory card in this camera before, you usually don't need to format it. But if it's a new, unformatted card, you should format it the first time you put it in. It's a good idea to format cards occasionally to clear out leftover data from previous shots, which can otherwise take up space on the card.

To format the card:

1. Go to the main menu

2. Choose "Format Card"

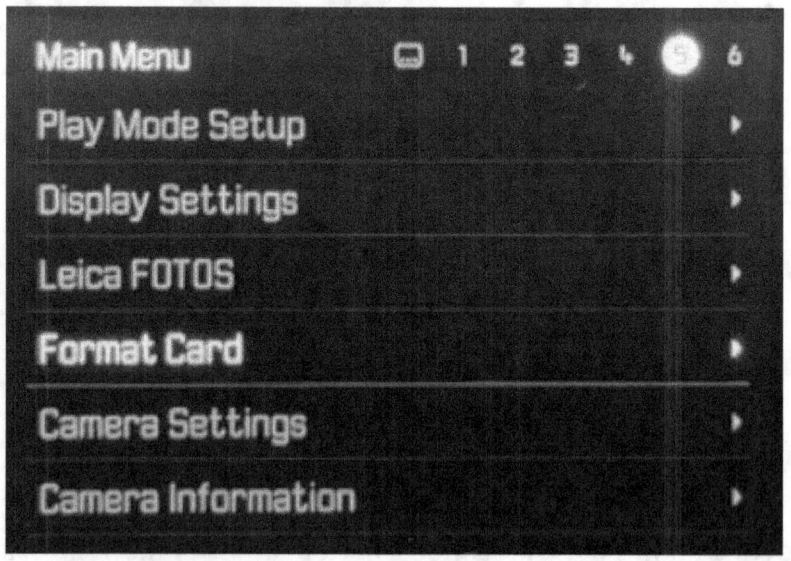

3. Confirm your selection

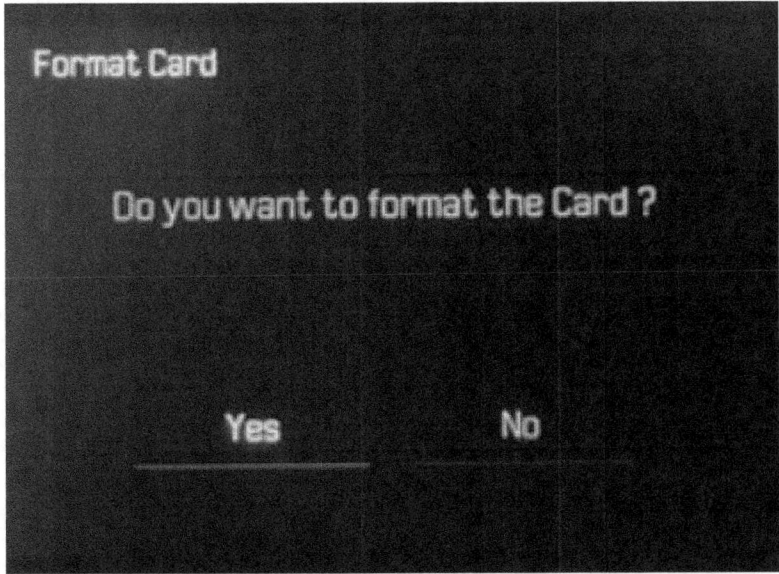

4. Wait for the lower status LED to flash during the formatting process.

Note:

- Don't turn off the camera when it's sending data.

- If you format the memory card, you'll lose all the data on it, and the protection for individual photos won't stop it. So, regularly move your images to a safe place like a computer.

- Formatting won't immediately erase everything on the card, just the directory. You can recover data with software unless it gets overwritten.

- If you formatted the card on a different device, like a computer, format it again in the camera.

Data Structure

Folder Structure

The pictures on the memory cards are stored in folders that are created automatically. The first three characters are numbers representing the folder number, and the last five characters are letters representing the folder name. The initial folder is named "100LEICA," each subsequent folder gets the next available number, up to a maximum of 999 folders.

File Structure

The files in these folders have names with eleven characters. In the beginning, the first file is named "L1000001.XXX", the second "L1000002.XXX", and so on. The first letter, "L," represents the camera brand. The first three characters show the folder number (numbers). The next four digits indicate the file number in sequence. When the file number reaches 9999, a new folder is made, and the numbering restarts from 0001. The last three characters after the dot show the file format (MOV or MP4).

Note: If you insert a memory card not formatted in this camera, it starts numbering files from 0001. If the card already has a higher-numbered file, it continues from there. A message shows up when reaching folder 999 or file 9999, signaling you to reset all numbering. To reset, format the card and immediately reset the frame number for the folder number to be 100 again.

Edit File Names

1. Go to the main menu and choose "Camera Settings."

2. Select "Edit File Name," and a keyboard will pop up.

3. The default file name starts with the letter "L." You can only change this first letter.

4. Type in the letter you want and press "Confirm."

Note:

- When you rename a file, the new name stays for all the following pictures until you change it again. The number order stays the same unless you create a new folder.

- If you reset to factory settings, the first letter of the file name will always be "L." You can't use lowercase letters.

Creating a New Folder

1. Go to the main menu and choose "Camera Settings."

2. Pick "Reset Image Numbering," and a message will pop up.

3. Decide whether to make a new folder (choose "Yes") or cancel (choose "No").

Note: When you make a new folder like this, the first letter of its name stays the same, but the numbers for the files inside start over at 0001.

CONCLUSION

The Leica Q3 stands as a testament to the ongoing pursuit of excellence in photography and videography. Combining high-quality craftsmanship, an iconic design, and user-friendly functionality, this third generation of the Leica Q series marks a significant evolution in the realm of fixed focal length full-frame cameras.

With its groundbreaking BSI-CMOS sensor featuring Triple-Resolution-Technology, the Leica Q3 empowers users to capture images with exceptional detail and flexibility. The fast Leica Summilux 28 mm f/1.7 ASPH. lens, complemented by integrated macro capabilities and an extended digital zoom, expands creative possibilities in both photography and videography.

The autofocus system, equipped with hybrid technology and phase detection, ensures rapid and precise focusing, enabling the capture of sharp and brilliant images. The addition of a tiltable high-resolution touchscreen, combined with seamless connectivity via Bluetooth and Wi-Fi, enhances the user experience and opens up new horizons for creative expression.

You've crossed the finish line of your Leica Q3 User Guide. Now, your camera's secrets are yours to unlock, and you're ready to capture the world in stunning ways. But remember, this guide is just the launchpad.

The real magic of the Leica Q3 isn't in the pages, it's in the moments you freeze, the stories you tell, and the feelings you evoke through your pictures. Use what you've learned to play, explore, and find your own unique voice. Trust your gut, be bold, and don't be afraid to bend the rules. Think of the Q3 as more than just a camera; it's an extension of you, a silent partner on your visual adventures.